W9-BZX-350

JOB

A MAN OF HEROIC ENDURANCE

An Interactive Study Guide

BASED ON THE BOOK BY

CHARLES R. SWINDOLL

Produced in association with CREATIVE MINISTRIES
Insight for Living

W PUBLISHING GROUP
A Division of Thomas Nelson Publishers
Since 1798

www.wpublishinggroup.com

Job: A Man of Heroic Endurance
An Interactive Study Guide

By Charles R. Swindoll

© 2004 Charles R. Swindoll, Inc. All rights reserved. No portion of this book may be reproduced, stored in a retrieval system, or transmitted in any form or by any means—electronic, mechanical, photocopy, recording, or any other—except for brief quotations in printed reviews, without the prior permission of the publisher.

Published by W Publishing Group, A Division of Thomas Nelson, Inc., P. O. Box 141000, Nashville, Tennessee, 37214.

Unless otherwise indicated, Scripture quotations are from the *New American Standard Bible* (NASB). Copyright © 1960, 1962, 1963, 1968, 1971, 1972, 1973, 1975, 1977, 1995 by The Lockman Foundation. Used by permission. (www.Lockman.org).

Scripture quotations identified NIV are from the *Holy Bible,* New International Version. Copyright © 1973, 1978, 1984 International Bible Society. Used by permission of Zondervan Bible Publishers. *NIV* and *New International Version* are registered in the United States Patent and Trademark Office by International Bible Society.

Scripture quotations identified MSG are taken from *The Message,* copyright © 1992, 1994, 1995, 1996, 2000, 2001, 2002 by NavPress Publishing Group. Used by permission. All rights reserved.

ISBN 0-8499-4501-1

Printed in the United States of America
03 04 05 06 vg 9 8 7 6 5 4 3 2 1

Job: A Man of Heroic Endurance
An Interactive Study Guide

Charles R. Swindoll has devoted his life to the clear, practical teaching and application of God's Word and His grace. A pastor at heart, Chuck has served as senior pastor to congregations in Texas, Massachusetts, and California. He currently pastors Stonebriar Community Church in Frisco, Texas, but Chuck's listening audience extends far beyond a local church body. As a leading program in Christian broadcasting, *Insight for Living* airs in major Christian radio markets around the world, reaching churched and unchurched people groups in languages they can understand. Chuck's extensive writing ministry has also served the body of Christ worldwide, and his leadership as president and now chancellor of Dallas Theological Seminary has helped prepare and equip a new generation for ministry. Chuck and Cynthia, his partner in life and ministry, have four grown children and ten grandchildren.

Based on the original outlines, charts, and transcripts of Charles R. Swindoll's sermons, the interactive study guide text was developed and written by the creative ministries department of Insight for Living.

Editor-in-Chief: Cynthia Swindoll

Managing Editor: Brian Goins

Study Guide Writer: Marla Alupoaicei

Editors: Greg Smith and Amy Snedaker

Original outlines, charts, and transcripts:
Copyright © 2002 by Charles R. Swindoll. All rights reserved.

Contents

CONTENTS

Contents

Acknowledgments

As with most projects, this effort required a team. We would like to thank David Moberg and the W Publishing Group for their wisdom, leadership, and vision to minister to the needs of people.

Special thanks to Mary Hollingsworth for her keen eye, professionalism, servant's heart, and gracious attitude as our teams worked together to meet tight writing, editing, and print deadlines.

Patty Crowley, thank you for your invaluable input as you copyedited this guide.

We also want to thank Kathryn Murray for tackling the monumental task of designing and typesetting our first interactive study guide.

Each of you did far more than we could have asked or imagined. We trust that your unwavering desire to communicate God's truth will minister to each person who reads this guide. We appreciate your commitment to making the Word of God and its application accessible to people all over the world. Together, we cling to God's promise that His Word will never return void, but will put down roots and bring forth fruit in the lives of countless people.

—CREATIVE MINISTRIES, INSIGHT FOR LIVING

A Letter from Chuck

IF SOMEONE ASKED YOU TO DESCRIBE the book of Job, what would you say? You might call it a story that illustrates the unfairness of life. Or a treatise on the depth of human suffering. Maybe you'd describe it as the portrait of a man who served God yet lost everything. And you'd be right! All of these themes surface in the book of Job. However, Job offers us so much more than the heart-wrenching story of one man's suffering. It provides us with a vast treasure trove of God's truth that we can apply to our lives when our circumstances reach the limits of our own endurance.

In this study, we'll take up our pickaxes and mine valuable treasures from Job's life. We'll see this righteous man emerge as a diamond in the rough whom the Lord selected and shaped for His purposes. Most importantly, we'll discover that the main focus of the book is not Job's suffering, but his indomitable faith in God.

So join us on our journey as we enter Job's world and see how he clung to his faith in God despite the worst possible circumstances. Travel with us as we walk with him through his trials and his eventual triumph, when God rewarded him for passing every test that Satan sent his way. Hopefully, Job's courageous faith will encourage you to lean hard on the Lord in every situation, knowing that He "causes all things to work together for good to those who love God, to those who are called according to His purpose" (Romans 8:28).

Charles R. Swindoll

How to Use This Study Guide

T HE GOAL OF THIS WORKBOOK IS SIMPLE: You will dig deeply into truths to apply them personally to every aspect of your life. This interactive workbook serves as an ideal tool for personal devotions, small-group studies, and church curriculum.

Personal Devotions—When your one-on-one time with God needs direction, this interactive workbook will guide you on the path toward greater wisdom, knowledge, and spiritual maturity.

Small-Group Bible Studies—When your small group desires to lay biblical foundations and build authentic community, this study guide provides you with a blueprint for learning God's Word and encouraging each other as you live together under His construction.

Church Curriculum—When your church body needs a resource that offers real answers to tough questions, this workbook will provide biblical truth, straight answers, and life-application questions in an exciting, conversation-stimulating format.

Every chapter in the workbook is composed of two primary sections:

Treasures from the Text—This section guides you through the biblical text. It contains teaching, application, reflection, and questions that will help you glean important principles and truths from God's Word.

Nuggets of Wisdom—This portion of the workbook provides powerful application points to help you focus on God's principles and incorporate what you've learned into your everyday life.

HOW TO USE THIS STUDY GUIDE

In addition to what you'll gain from the two main sections in each chapter, you will find five "special feature" categories interspersed throughout the guide. These will help you further unpack the intricacies of Scripture and cultivate intimacy with the Almighty.

 *Digging Deeper*—This portion of the workbook offers you deeper insight into certain aspects of Christian theology and practice. It will help you focus on subject areas of particular interest raised in the chapters.

 Getting to the Root—In this section, you'll learn the origins and meanings of Hebrew and Greek words from the original biblical text.

 In Other Words—This section provides practical, applicable quotes from various authors, as well as interactive questions to help you absorb and apply the truth you glean from the author's insights.

 Taking Truth to Heart—In this section, you'll have the opportunity for personal reflection as you integrate principles from God's Word and the workbook chapter into your life.

 Windows to the Ancient World—Here, you'll find fascinating historical and cultural gems that will expand your understanding of the customs and practices of the biblical world as they relate to the text.

May God's Word be a lamp to your feet and light to your path as you discover and apply its truths!

1 Setting the Stage for Disaster

Job 1:1–12

> The LORD said to Satan, "Have you considered My servant Job? For there is no one like him on the earth, a blameless and upright man, fearing God and turning away from evil."
>
> —Job 1:8

SOMETIMES LIFE JUST ISN'T FAIR. One moment, we're soaring gracefully on the gossamer wings of success; the next, life's hardships knock the wind out of us and send us sprawling. Even when we're serving the Lord to the best of our ability, we face disappointing setbacks and staggering losses that make us ask, "Why, God?"

No one would deny that our lives are punctuated with hardship, heartaches, and headaches. Most of us have learned to face the reality that life is difficult. But *unfair?* When we face an unfair situation, a rush of emotion kicks in deep within us. Our fervent desire for justice tends to override our ability to endure unfair circumstances.

An incident from the 2002 Olympic Winter Games provides a powerful example. Imagine that you've been born and reared in Canada, and you've been training as an ice skater for most of your life. Every day, you dream of making it to the Olympics. Skating is difficult. You fall more times than you can remember, but every fall teaches you another lesson, and every day you work on perfecting your technique. You hire a well-known skating coach and find a skating partner, who is also from your homeland. Over time, you and your partner learn to skate magnificently together, and you work toward your mutual dream of competing at the Salt Lake City 2002 Winter Olympics.

Finally, your dream becomes a reality. Your Olympic moment arrives! As the commentator reads your names, you and your partner slide smoothly onto the ice and wait for the music to begin. You perform your routine perfectly, better than you've ever done it. And you know in your hearts as you finish that it was a gold-medal performance. Both of you are ecstatic—until you see the scores. Your heart sinks. As you read the numbers, you realize that you'll get the silver medal and another couple less deserving than you will win the gold. At that moment, life is difficult.

In a few hours' time, however, you find out that the scoring was tainted—the competition was fixed by a dishonest judge. Suddenly, "difficult" becomes "unfair," and that's a whole different matter. Once you learn that the judging was unfair, you can't tolerate the thought of accepting the silver medal. Crushed, you wait in fearful anticipation while the Olympic committee investigates the problem. Thankfully, the committee eventually rules in your favor. You and your partner rejoice as you finally receive the Olympic gold. Justice is served!

This true saga bears striking similarities to that of Job. This godly man experienced situations that were not only difficult, but from our point of view, they seem downright unfair. Job lived through some of the most excruciating trials imaginable, facing one painful test after another in the crucible of life. He endured horrors that few of us have ever experienced. But his story has a happy ending as well. Job showed himself faithful, and the Lord eventually restored Job's health, his family, and his fortunes. Job emerged from his suffering as purified gold, reflecting the image of God more clearly than ever.

In Other Words

In his best-selling book *Disappointment with God,* Phillip Yancey writes:

> If you had asked me when I began my study what the book of Job was about, I would have been quick to respond. *Job? Everybody knows what Job is about. It's the Bible's most complete treatment of the problem of suffering. It's about terrible grief and bewildering pain.*
>
> . . . I now believe I misread the book—or, more accurately, didn't take into account the entire book. Despite the fact that all but a few pages of Job deal with the problem of pain, I am coming to the conclusion that Job is not really about the problem of pain. Suffering contributes the ingredients of the story, not its central theme. Just as a cake is not about eggs, flour, milk, and shortening, but uses those ingredients in the process of creating a cake, Job is not "about" suffering; it merely uses such ingredients in its larger story, which concerns even more important questions, cosmic questions. Seen as a whole, Job is primarily about *faith* in its starkest form.[1]

Incredible, isn't it? The book that we thought centered on suffering actually focuses on faith. As we follow Job on his journey, we'll see his faith severely tested. Stripped of his family and his possessions, he stood beside ten fresh graves on a windswept hill, crying out to God with some of life's most difficult questions.

No doubt, you're asking God a few questions yourself. Perhaps you're reeling from the unexpected illness or death of a beloved family member. Maybe your spouse has deserted you, leaving an enormous void in your life. You may be dealing with a debilitating personal illness, or maybe the loss of your job or failure of your business has left you in a financial crisis.

The book of Job contains wisdom and godly principles to help you address every painful circumstance. Remember, this isn't a book of trite, sugar-coated sayings. It holds real-life answers to your real-life questions! And best of all, despite all the pain that Job endured, the book ends well as he emerges from his suffering with a deeper understanding of God's sovereignty, justice, and love. As you come to terms with Job's story, you'll gain hope that you, too, can pass the faith tests that life sends your way.

TREASURES FROM THE TEXT

Job's Character

Let's begin by getting to know Job. The biblical text introduces him this way:

> There was a man in the land of Uz whose name was Job; and that man was blameless, upright, fearing God and turning away from evil. (Job 1:1)

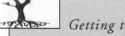

Getting to the Root

The word *blameless* comes from the Hebrew root meaning "to be complete." This term describes Job's spiritual maturity and the integrity of his inner being. *Upright* means "straight" or "right" in Hebrew and indicates that Job's attitudes and actions were in line with God's will and His ways.[2]

Job wasn't perfect, but he shunned moral evil and made his spiritual life his first priority. He handled his business affairs with integrity. He managed his servants and his flocks with compassion and care. His family and friends loved, respected, honored, and admired him. That's just the kind of person Job was!

Why do you think the author emphasizes the fact that Job was "blameless and upright?" Do you know (or know of) anyone like this?

Job's Possessions and Family

Seven sons and three daughters were born to him. His possessions also were 7,000 sheep, 3,000 camels, 500 yoke of oxen, 500 female donkeys, and very many servants; and that man was the greatest of all the men of the east. His sons used to go and hold a feast in the house of each one on his day, and they would send and invite their three sisters to eat and drink with them. (Job 1:2–4)

How would you describe Job's circumstances at this point in his life?

Job's Role as a Father

When the days of feasting had completed their cycle, Job would send and consecrate them, rising up early in the morning and offering burnt offerings according to the number of them all; for Job said, "Perhaps my sons have sinned and cursed God in their hearts." Thus Job did continually. (Job 1:5)

According to verses 2 through 5, what kind of a father was Job? How did he prioritize spiritual values and responsibilities within his family?

Job performed the role of a priest for his family, offering burnt offerings at the end of every feast cycle. He cared not only about his own spiritual walk, but also about those of his wife and children. He took seriously his obligation for offering sin sacrifices, presenting ten special offerings in case his sons or daughters had secretly cursed God. As we work our way through the book of Job, we'll see the themes of cursing and blessing emerge as key motifs.

Satan's Wager

Now there was a day when the sons of God came to present themselves before the LORD, and Satan also came among them. The LORD said to Satan, "From where do you come?" Then Satan answered the LORD and said, "From roaming about on the earth and walking around on it." (Job 1:6–7)

Be of sober spirit, be on the alert. Your adversary, the devil, prowls around like a roaring lion, seeking someone to devour. (1 Peter 5:8)

Getting to the Root

Satan's name comes from the Hebrew verb *satan*, meaning "to be or act as an adversary." In Greek, his name is translated *diabolos*, meaning "the accuser."[3]

The fact that Satan approached God's throne along with the holy angels reminds us that he's not a small, helpless imp with a red body and a pitchfork who sits on our shoulder, whispering ugly little nothings into our ears. That's a medieval caricature that Satan would love us to believe.

Actually, Lucifer once served as the most attractive, brilliant, powerful archangel ever. His name literally means "star of the morning." But when he tried to usurp God's power, the Lord cast him down from heaven with the other rebellious angels, and Lucifer became known as Satan.

We sometimes forget that Satan has not lost his ability to tempt. He hasn't lost his beauty, his brilliance, or his power. He continually seeks to destroy us through his evil workings behind the scenes. Satan and his demons may be invisible most of the time, but they're *real*. They have personalities and wills, and they're absolutely committed to trying to destroy God's people and ruin God's plan.

Read James 4:6–8. What is the heart attitude that James indicates will protect you against Satan's attacks? How can you show this attitude in relating to God?

Job's Role as God's Servant

> The LORD said to Satan, "Have you considered My servant Job? For there is no one like him on the earth, a blameless and upright man, fearing God and turning away from evil." (Job 1:8)

In all the Bible, God refers to only eleven people or groups as "My servant": Abraham (Genesis 26:24); Moses (Numbers 12:7–8); Caleb (Numbers 14:24); David (2 Samuel 3:18); Isaiah (Isaiah 20:3); Eliakim (Isaiah 22:20); the nation of Israel (Isaiah 41:8); Nebuchadnezzar, king of Babylon (Jeremiah 25:9); Zerubbabel (Haggai 2:23); the Branch, Jesus Christ (Zechariah 3:8); and Job (Job 1:8; 2:3). Every time God calls someone "My servant," He illustrates the intimate spiritual relationship He has with that person. This title also indicates submission and a willingness to be used according to God's purposes.

What aspects of Job's life indicate that he was God's servant?

At this point in your life, do you think God would call you "My servant"? If not, what attitudes or actions in your life need to change?

Satan's Accusations

> Then Satan answered the LORD, "Does Job fear God for nothing? Have You not made a hedge about him and his house and all that he has, on every side? You have blessed the work of his hands, and his possessions have increased in the land. But put forth Your hand now and touch all that he has; he will surely curse You to Your face." (Job 1:9–11)

How did Satan accuse God in these verses?

What accusations did Satan make against Job?

> Then the LORD said to Satan, "Behold, all that he has is in your power, only do not put forth your hand on him." So Satan departed from the presence of the LORD. (Job 1:12)

Why do you think the Lord accepted Satan's wager and allowed him to test Job?

How did the Lord *protect* Job, according to this verse?

Windows to the Ancient World

God called Job "blameless and upright, fearing God and turning away from evil" (see Job 1:8; 2:3). But who exactly *was* Job? Where did he live? Did he write the book of Job himself, and if so, when? We'll answer these questions and more as we dig deeper into the background of this faithful man.

We're told that Job lived in Uz, a land in the upper Arabian desert (see Job 1:1; Jeremiah 25:20; Lamentations 4:21). God blessed him with a wife, ten children, and vast holdings of livestock. But his faithfulness and wisdom were his greatest assets.

Scholars offer several suggestions regarding the authorship of the book of Job. Many believe that Job himself wrote it. Others propose Elihu, Moses, Solomon, Hezekiah, Isaiah, Ezra, or an anonymous author.

If Job wrote the book, he most likely lived between 2100 and 1900 B.C., since he seemed to share a tradition and lifestyle similar to that of the biblical patriarchs (Abraham, Isaac, and Jacob) who lived around this time. This date is supported by Job's longevity of about 210 years, the fact that his wealth was measured in livestock, and the description of his position as priest of his family. In addition, the discovery of parts of the book of Job among the Dead Sea Scrolls suggests an early date. If this date for the writing of Job is accurate, then Job was the first Bible book written.

Job falls into the general category of wisdom literature, along with Psalms, Proverbs, Ecclesiastes, and the Song of Solomon. The wisdom books illustrate how God works in the arena of human experience.

How would you define wisdom?

In Scripture, the most commonly used terms for "wisdom" are *hokmah* in Hebrew and *sophia* in Greek. Both terms offer a powerful, yet concise definition of wisdom—"skill in godly living." As we learn more about Job's wisdom and faith in the face of trials, we'll glean principles that we can use to increase our own skill in godly living.

NUGGETS OF WISDOM

From the first twelve verses of the book of Job, we can glean four principles to apply to our lives. First, *we can't see our enemy, but he's real, and he's powerful.* His strategies will play tricks on your mind. His ultimate goal is to conquer you and bring you down. He wants to ruin your testimony and destroy your life. If that means ruining your family relationships, he'll go there. If it means tempting you sexually, he'll do it. If it means convincing you to cut a shady business deal, he'll try. So be on your guard!

How can you guard yourself spiritually, physically, and emotionally against temptation in those areas of your life in which you are feeling the most pressure?

Second, *we don't deserve trials, yet God permits them.* We don't always understand why, but God allows suffering to happen in this world. Yet when life's storms threaten to drown us in a sea of despair, we can seek refuge in the Rock. The Bible also says that, like a mother hen, God protects us in the shadow of His wings (see Psalm 17:8). Over time, we learn to recognize that trials have a positive purpose in our lives. They teach us to depend fully on God.

What principles is God teaching you through your current trials?

Third, *we don't always understand God's plan, but it is best.* If we understood everything about God's plan, He wouldn't be God. We must learn to accept both positive and negative situations as a part of life instead of becoming bitter and blaming God. Nothing touches our lives that has not first passed through the hands of the Lord. He is fully sovereign, and He loves us. So when a dark cloud seems to blot out the sun on your life's horizon, remind yourself that your Father created you and desires the best for you as His child.

What steps can you take to come to better terms with the mystery of God's plan?

Fourth, *we experience circumstances that we could not anticipate.* Sometimes we think that if we love God, read His Word, and follow His commands, then we'll reap only happiness and blessings from life. But we're wrong! Worldly happiness and spiritual joy aren't the same thing. We're told in Scripture that seeking after worldly happiness is a losing battle (see Ecclesiastes 2:1–2). But when we place our trust in our heavenly Father, we have peace and a true joy that lasts, no matter our circumstances. Psalm 126:5 promises us that "Those who sow in tears shall reap with joyful shouting." We're also reminded that "a joyful heart is good medicine" (Proverbs 17:22).

How can you prioritize the pursuit of godliness, true joy, and spiritual maturity in your life instead of worldly happiness?

Life may be unfair, but God is righteous and loving. Though our circumstances may appear adverse, *they will work together for good.* Romans 8:28 reads, "And we know that God causes all things to work together for good to those who love God, to those who are called according to His purpose." That's a solid promise from God's Word!

Reeling and Recovering from Devastating News

2

Job 1:13–22

> The LORD gave and the LORD has taken away.
> Blessed be the name of the LORD.
>
> — Job 1:21

EVERY SITUATION HAS TWO VERY DIFFERENT PERSPECTIVES: God's and ours. In the first two chapters of Job, we get a glimpse of God's viewpoint on the events to follow. Job, however, had only his limited human perspective to guide him. Completely in the dark concerning Satan's wager, he had no idea why he was suddenly facing such fiery trials.

Phillip Yancey describes Job's position this way:

> It helps to think of the book of Job as a mystery play, a "whodunit" detective story. Before the play itself begins, we in the audience get a sneak preview, as if we have showed up early for a press conference in which the director explains his work (chapters 1–2). He relates the plot and describes the main characters, then tells us in advance who did what in the play, and why. In fact, he solves every mystery in the play except one: how will the main character respond? Will Job trust God or deny him?
>
> . . . We know the answer to the "whodunit" questions, but the star detective, Job, does not. He spends all his time on stage trying to discover what we already know. He scratches himself with shards of pottery and asks, "Why me? What did I do wrong? What is God trying to tell me?"
>
> . . . Why . . . is Job suffering? Not for punishment. Far from it—he has been selected as the principal player in a great contest of the heavens."[1]

Little did Job know that his faithfulness had become the focus of a cosmic struggle between God and Satan. God won in the end, but Job endured some excruciating losses and severe faith tests before the Lord finally restored him. As Job entered the dark tunnel of tough trials, he must have wondered if he would ever again see the light.

Getting to the Root
James, the half-brother of Jesus, wrote, "You have heard of the endurance of Job . . ." (Jas. 5:11). The Greek word for endurance, *hupomonē*, means "to tolerate or suffer,"[2] as a person who patiently bears a load.

TREASURES FROM THE TEXT

Job Loses His Oxen, Donkeys, and Servants

> Now on the day when his sons and his daughters were eating and drinking wine in their oldest brother's house, a messenger came to Job and said, "The oxen were plowing and the donkeys feeding beside them, and the Sabeans attacked and took them. They also slew the servants with the edge of the sword, and I alone have escaped to tell you." (Job 1:13–15)

The first wave had begun. Many of Job's animals and servants (and the financial stability they provided) were suddenly torn from his hands.

How do you imagine Job felt when he heard the messenger's report?

Think back to a time when you received unexpected bad news. What were the circumstances? How did you respond?

Job Loses His Sheep, Camels, and More Servants

> While he was still speaking, another also came and said, "The fire of God fell from heaven and burned up the sheep and the servants and consumed them, and I alone have escaped to tell you." While he was still speaking, another also came and said, "The Chaldeans formed three bands and made a raid on the camels and took them and slew the servants with the edge of the sword, and I alone have escaped to tell you." (Job 1:16–17)

Job hadn't even absorbed the magnitude of his first loss before the next one confronted him. The individual waves of trials escalated to become an enormous tidal wave, destroying everything in its path.

Put yourself in Job's place. As he faced calamity after calamity, what thoughts must have gone through his mind?

Have you ever faced a tidal wave of difficult trials? If so, what were the circumstances?

How did God use these trials to strengthen your faith?

Job Loses His Sons and Daughters

> While he was still speaking, another also came and said, "Your sons and your daughters were eating and drinking wine in their oldest brother's house, and behold, a great wind came from across the wilderness and struck the four corners of the house, and it fell on the young people and they died, and I alone have escaped to tell you." (Job 1:18–19)

Each wave of tragedy had threatened to drown Job, but now this . . . unthinkable. The previous disasters faded in importance as he heard the report of the loss of all ten of his children.

How would you expect Job to react after hearing the heart-wrenching news that they had died?

How do you think you would react if you received the same bad news?

Job's Response to His Calamity

> Then Job arose and tore his robe and shaved his head, and he fell to the ground and worshiped. (Job 1:20)

14

Job first responded to this overwhelming chain of events by tearing his robe and shaving his head, outwardly demonstrating his grief. You might think that after taking these steps, he would lash out at God for letting such terrible calamities befall him. Instead, he did the opposite: He fell prostrate on the ground and *worshiped God.*

He said,
>   "Naked I came from my mother's womb,
>   And naked I shall return there.
>   The LORD gave and the LORD has taken away.
>   Blessed be the name of the LORD."
> Through all this Job did not sin nor did he blame God. (Job 1:21–22)

Everything Job owned went up in smoke, and all of his children died in a single moment! A quick, brutal sweep of devastation reduced this godly man to a mass of brokenness and grief. Yet, amazingly, Job did not blame God. Instead, he chose to follow adversity with adoration and woe with worship. He refused to give in to bitterness and, despite the horrible catastrophes that had occurred in his life, he did not accuse God of wrongdoing (see Job 2:10).

Have you ever lost a friend or family member due to a sudden tragedy? If so, what feelings did you experience as you went through the grieving process?

How did you respond to God during this time? How would you characterize your faith during this difficult trial?

What do you think enabled Job to have such a godly response to such deep and undeserved suffering?

What do Job's experiences teach us about trusting God's sovereignty?

Taking Truth to Heart

Like Job, we never know when we will have to face a crisis that makes us realize how fiercely we depend on God. For example, few Americans could have predicted the wave of sinister terrorist acts that resulted in the loss of thousands of innocent lives on September 11, 2001.

The twin towers that once added breathtaking height and elegance to the New York City skyline are now conspicuous by their absence. In Washington, D.C., an entire wing of the Pentagon was destroyed. A peaceful site near a wooded section in southwest Pennsylvania has been scarred forever. Yet, in the wake of these horrendous events, one name emerged: Todd Beamer. Many others performed heroic deeds, but the story of this particular individual stands out in bold relief.

The events of Todd's life that fateful morning may be familiar to you. The flight he had boarded, United Airlines Flight 93, was hijacked by terrorists sometime after takeoff. From the hijacked plane, Todd used his cell phone to call the GTE Communications Center in Oakbrook, Illinois. He spoke with one of the supervisors, Lisa Jefferson, about the situation. His carefully guarded words were sometimes calm, sometimes anguished, sometimes mixed with tears as he asked Ms. Jefferson to tell his wife and children that he loved them. Finally, Todd asked her to pray the Lord's Prayer with him. After that prayer, Todd's last words were firm: "Are you guys ready? Let's roll!" And indeed they did.

Todd and others on board created and carried out a plan to confront the hijackers and divert the plane to keep it from hitting its target—most likely, the White House. Thanks to Todd and his fellow passengers, the terrorists were kept from accomplishing their objective. The plane crashed into a meadow in Pennsylvania, killing everyone on board. A faithful husband and father, Todd left behind two children and his wife, also named Lisa, who was expecting their third child.

Todd Beamer wasn't physically trained to fight terrorists. He was just a passenger on a plane! But when placed in a terrifying situation, he sacrificed his own life to save others, and by doing so, Todd became a hero.[3] His actions bring to mind these words from the nineteenth-century poet Henry Wadsworth Longfellow:

> The heights by great men reached and kept
> Were not attained by sudden flight,
> But they, while their companions slept
> Were toiling upward in the night.[4]

We learn an important lesson from the experience of Todd Beamer. To respond with heroic effort and patient endurance when disaster strikes—and it does in every life—we must be prepared beforehand. When tragedy hits, it's too late to start training ourselves spiritually and emotionally. Instead, we must pursue the spiritual disciplines *now*. When we spend time daily in prayer, worship, and Bible study, we anchor our minds and hearts in God and His Word. As a result, the Lord will build our faith, increase our knowledge, and raise our level of spiritual maturity so that we're better prepared to face trials when they inevitably come.

How would you describe a "heroic" person? What qualities does a true hero possess?

What daily preparations are you making to face the future trials that will come in your life?

Digging Deeper

The book of Job delves deeply into the subject of *theodicy*—the relationship of divine justice to human suffering. This term represents the combination of two Greek words: *theos,* meaning "God," and *dike,* meaning "justice."[5] The suffering of mankind represents one of life's greatest and most difficult mysteries. In order to gain a godly perspective on our suffering, we must not only acknowledge God's sovereignty, we also need to understand the difference between God's *active will* and His *permissive will.*

God often chooses to step into time, working miracles, saving lives, and dramatically answering our prayers. When He does so, He demonstrates His *active will.* He actively reaches into our lives to change our circumstances. In this way, He demonstrates His love, goodness, and mercy toward us.

But God is also just. When sin entered the world through Adam, suffering was part of the curse that he brought on mankind. God allowed this to happen as a result of man's willful disobedience. In so doing, He demonstrated His *permissive will.*

How does this apply to Job's situation? It means that God *allowed* Job's suffering at the hand of Satan, but He did not cause that suffering. The Lord loved Job intimately, and He allowed trials in Job's life that would help him grow and mature spiritually. Remember, God saw the future! He knew that Job had faith strong enough to pass every test that Satan would send his way.

Have you ever noticed that the word *justice* appears many times in the Bible, but the word *fairness* never appears? While life may not be fair sometimes, Scripture tells us that *God is always just.* When you face difficult struggles, keep in mind that God isn't punishing you or turning His back on you. In fact, He'll use your trials to draw you into closer fellowship with Himself.

If you faced a situation similar to that of Todd Beamer, how would you want to respond?

What changes do you need to make in your life in order to be prepared to overcome obstacles in the future?

Read the following passages. What does each say about the justice and righteousness of God?

Deuteronomy 32:4

Nehemiah 9:32–34

Isaiah 45:21

Romans 9:14

How do fairness and justice differ?

NUGGETS OF WISDOM

Consider the lesson of this story of a man who, like Job, experienced a great loss:

> Several years ago, a friend of mine who lived in the Santa Barbara Canyon area of California went through a frightening ordeal. One parched summer, fire swept through the region devouring thousands of acres of forest and destroying countless homes in the canyon. His home sat at the base of the long canyon. . . . He could see the flames and smoke in the distance and knew he only had a short while before his home would become engulfed in fire. He hurriedly made a list of those possessions he most wanted to save. As it turned out, he didn't have time to grab any of them. When the whole ordeal was over, he stood looking at the smoldering heap that was once his home. All that remained was the list he had clutched in his hand. . . .
>
> [His family] lost everything, except of course the useless list of items they thought they couldn't do without. The fire, though unbelievably devastating, became a catalyst for changing them into a closer, more grateful family.[6]

If you were to lose all of your possessions in a fire or other disaster, how do you think you would respond?

Which of your possessions would you miss the most?

How do you think you would be changed if you lost the people and things you hold dear?

One of the greatest lessons we learn from Job is that "you can't take it with you." Job recognized that everything in his care was on loan from God. He didn't own it; God did. Job realized that God had given him the gifts of children, possessions, and good health, and if the Lord chose to take those gifts away, that was His prerogative.

Corrie ten Boom once said, "I've learned that we must hold everything loosely, because when I grip it tightly, it hurts when the Father pries my fingers loose and takes it from me!"[7] God allows us to be stewards of our families, our cars, our homes, and our businesses. The problem arises when we think we own these things, but *they actually own us.*

Are you clinging too tightly to certain people or possessions in your life right now? If so, who or what are they?

Write out a prayer to God now, releasing these people and things into His care.

Because God is sovereign, we know that we can trust His purposes in allowing suffering in our lives. And because He is our loving heavenly Father, not willing that any should perish, we can trust His heart. Remember, life may be unfair, but God isn't. When disaster strikes, He'll be there with open arms.

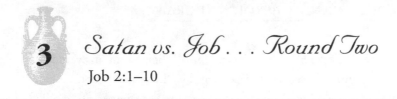

3 Satan vs. Job . . . Round Two

Job 2:1–10

> In all this Job did not sin with his lips.
>
> —Job 2:10

O<small>N THE EVENING</small> of Monday, September 10, 2001, thousands of workers left their offices in the World Trade Center to head home. They rushed onto packed subways, using their commute to plan ahead for the next day—making phone calls, adding appointments to their PDAs, and creating to-do lists.

Many of them came in early the next morning to begin work—with no inkling that American Airlines Flight 11 was heading straight for the North Tower, soon to hit the building with massive force. Eighteen minutes later, those in the South Tower would feel the jarring impact of United Airlines Flight 175 as it crashed through the skyscraper's steel infrastructure. Soon after, another plane would plunge into the Pentagon, and hijackers would steer yet another plane toward their target in Washington, D.C. Would the terror ever stop?

Job must have asked the same question as wave after wave of calamity crashed over his once-placid life. Part of Satan's strategy was to hit Job while he was down. The cruel deceiver had already snatched away all of Job's possessions, leaving him with nothing but his wife, a few friends, and his faith in God. Now, Satan was about to inflict upon Job the most terrifying and painful trial of all: the loss of his good health.

TREASURES FROM THE TEXT

Satan Appears Again before God

Again there was a day when the sons of God came to present themselves before the LORD, and Satan also came among them to present himself before the LORD.

The LORD said to Satan, "Where have you come from?" Then Satan answered the LORD and said, "From roaming about on the earth and walking around on it." The LORD said to Satan, "Have you considered My servant Job? For there is no one like him on the earth, a blameless and upright man fearing God and turning away from evil. And he still holds fast his integrity, although you incited Me against him to ruin him without cause." (Job 2:1–3)

This section mirrors Job 1:6–8, but with an important exception: God's declaration that Job "still holds fast his integrity" (Job 2:3).

How does this statement influence your understanding of the book of Job?

What accusation did God make against Satan in Job 2:3?

Digging Deeper

The repartee between Satan and God in the book of Job raises a modern theological issue. You may have heard the term *dualism* swirling through certain theological circles. The dictionary defines *dualism* as "a doctrine that the universe is under the dominion of two opposing principles, one of which is good and the other evil."[1] Picture dualism as a kind of theological "Star Wars" in which both God ("the Force") and Satan ("the Dark Side") possess equally tremendous power.

Charles Dyer and Gene Merrill describe this tension in the following way:

While one should never minimize the power of the devil, it is important at the same time to recognize that his power can be exercised only to the extent that God permits it. This means that pain, illness, death, and even evil are somehow embraced within His sovereign plan. As difficult as this may be theologically, the alternative is to posit a dualism, a belief in a God of good and a god of evil, the two locked in irresolvable conflict. This, of course, is an idea completely foreign to God's Word.[2]

If Satan's power equaled that of God, we'd live in constant fear of Satan and his evil forces, and we could never be absolutely certain that God would triumph over Satan in the end. But thankfully, this isn't the case! *God created Satan to serve Him, and not the other way around.* God possesses greater power than Satan, and He defines and limits Satan's work on earth. The Almighty always has the final say!

Satan Replies to God's Challenge

Furious that his first scheme to destroy Job had failed, Satan paced back and forth before God's throne, trying to come up with a new plan of attack. Suddenly, he had a brilliantly insidious idea.

> Satan answered the LORD and said, "Skin for skin! Yes, all that a man has he will give for his life. However, put forth Your hand now, and touch his bone and his flesh; he will curse You to Your face." (Job 2:4–5)

What accusation did Satan make against God in this passage? What accusation did Satan make against Job?

Satan cunningly suggested that Job had remained faithful to God only because the assaults had destroyed Job's *possessions* and not his *person.* The deceiver hinted that once the attacks became more personal, Job's faith would fail. One Bible scholar addresses Satan's deceptive accusations this way:

> [Satan's] independent activity in this passage is mainly that of the spy of evil, of the accuser of man to God, especially the accuser of the pious, and he maintains the assertion that even their fear of God stems from personal interest.[3]

Satan's underlying accusation throughout the book of Job is that *Job served God simply because the Lord had blessed him so much*. The accuser snidely suggested that Job worshiped the Lord solely because of what he got out of the deal, and that once Job's blessings were gone, his loyalty to God would dry up as well. But as we continue to explore the depths of Job's character, we'll discover just how wrong Satan was.

God Responds to Satan's Ploy

> So the LORD said to Satan, "Behold, he is in your power, only spare his life." (Job 2:6)

What permission did God grant Satan here that He did not grant in chapter 1? (Compare Job 1:11–12 and 2:5–6.) Why do you think He did this?

Satan Afflicts Job's Flesh

> Then Satan went out from the presence of the Lord and smote Job with sore boils from the sole of his foot to the crown of his head. And he took a potsherd to scrape himself while he was sitting among the ashes. (Job 2:7–8)

The two Hebrew words for "sore boils" describe the festering sores that erupted as one of the Egyptian plagues (see Exodus 9:8–11 and Deuteronomy 28:27). Job's symptoms included these inflamed, ulcerous sores (Job 2:7); persistent itching (2:8), degenerative changes in facial skin (2:7, 12); loss of appetite (3:24); fear and depression (3:24–25); loss of strength (6:11); running sores with worms in them (7:5); difficulty breathing (9:18); darkness under the eyes (16:16); foul breath (19:17); loss of weight (19:20; 33:21); excruciating, continual pain (30:17); insomnia (30:27); blackened and peeling skin (30:30); and high fever with chills (30:30). In other words, Job became misery personified![4]

What kind of illness could have caused such excruciating symptoms? Scholars continue to debate this issue. Some suggest that Job had smallpox; others suggest elephantiasis, leprosy, psoriasis, or a disease called *pemphigus foliaceus*. Missionaries in primitive cultures have reported that patients with the latter manifest symptoms similar to Job's, and many of these patients also soothe their sores with ashes (see Job 2:8).[5]

Whatever his illness, Job resigned himself to living in filthy conditions at the city dump—the place where garbage and human excrement were burned. Warren Wiersbe writes:

> So abhorrent was Job's appearance that he fled society (Job 19:13–20) and went outside the city and sat on the ash heap. There the city's garbage was deposited and burned, and there the city's rejects lived, begging alms from whoever passed by. At the ash heap, dogs fought over something to eat, and the city's dung was brought and burned. The city's leading citizen was now living in abject poverty and shame.[6]

How humiliating! This man of God, who had once served as a respected judge at the city gates, now sat outside the city with lepers, beggars, and outcasts, scraping his itching, oozing sores with a piece of broken pottery (Job 2:8). In a short span of time, the "prince of Ur" had become a lowly pauper.

Have you ever dealt with a difficult or debilitating illness? If so, what was it?

How did it make you feel physically and emotionally? How did it affect you spiritually?

Isn't it strange that bad things always seem to happen to the wrong person? Struck with a horrible illness, Job was left asking the three-letter word *why?* "Why did such a thing have to happen? Why me? Why now?" This question is still being raised on every continent, in every country, in every city, in every home. Asking "why" remains a universal part of the human condition, but the answer often eludes us.

Yet somewhere in all of the asking, Job's story speaks to us. Remember, no better man lived in Job's day. Even God the Father had called him "upright and blameless"! Job had served his family as a faithful husband and a loving, devoted father. He had treated his servants fairly and managed his employees with integrity. His hard work and faithfulness to God had led to a prosperous period of his later life that he had planned to enjoy. He possessed plenty of livestock and goods to finance the dreams that he and his wife had for the future . . . until the bottom dropped out of his life.

Job must have hoped to awaken from this nightmare and find that it was only a bad dream. He faced one mind-numbing trial after another, and not only did he experience utter humiliation and crippling pain, but his own wife discouraged him.

Job's Wife Responds to His Suffering

> Then his wife said to him, "Do you still hold fast your integrity? Curse God and die!" (Job 2:9)

How do you think Job's wife felt at this point? Why do you think she offered the advice that she did?

Sharp words filled with bitterness and hurt emanated from Job's wife. But instead of treating her harshly, Job responded to her with a gentle reproach:

> But he said to her, "You speak as one of the foolish women speaks. Shall we indeed accept good from God and not accept adversity?" In all this Job did not sin with his lips. (Job 2:10)

In Hebrew, the second sentence of Job's response reads, "The good shall we accept from God and the trouble shall we not accept?" The word order emphasizes the phrases "the good" and "the trouble." Job asks this rhetorical question to help his wife think through the implications of her words. In essence, Job asks, "Doesn't God have the right to do what He thinks best? Isn't He the Potter? Aren't we the clay? Isn't He the Shepherd and we the sheep? Isn't He the Master and we the servants? Isn't that the way it works?"

Job's response brings to mind the words of a well-loved worship song:

> Change my heart, O God
> Make it ever true.
> Change my heart, O God
> May I be like You.
>
> You are the Potter
> I am the clay
> Mold me and make me
> This is what I pray.
>
> Change my heart, O God
> Make it ever true.
> Change my heart, O God
> May I be like You.[7]

Job knew that the clay does not ask the Potter, "What are you making?" And so he says, in effect, "No, sweetheart. Let's not do that. We serve a God who has the right to do whatever He wants and is never obligated to explain it or ask permission. God is no 'heavenly servant' of ours, waiting for the snap of our fingers. He is our Master! He has an extraordinary plan for our lives that is far beyond our comprehension." No doubt, Job's reminders helped to broaden his wife's perspective and turn her eyes back toward God.

We might be tempted to criticize "Mrs. Job" for offering such foolish advice to her husband. But before we do so, let's try to put ourselves in her place.

First, *she too had lost ten children.* The pain of losing even one precious child lingers for a lifetime. Can you imagine losing all ten at the same moment? Mrs. Job had already experienced heart-wrenching grief over the loss of her children. In her weakened emotional state, she couldn't bear to see her husband suffering, too.

Second, *she too had suffered the loss of their wealth and possessions.* Every wife with a well-to-do husband enjoys the blessings, benefits, perks, and pleasures that his financial security brings. But Mrs. Job's security and benefits had all disappeared—her home, her family, her possessions, her livestock, and her servants. In addition, her friends most likely scattered in horror at her plight. Mr. and Mrs. Job had been reduced to the same economic status—utter destitution.

Third, *she became the suffering, shamed wife of the most scorned man in the entire town.* For a long time, she had enjoyed being the wife of "the greatest of all the men of the east." She had enjoyed prestige. Power. Honor. Respect. Popularity. But all of these perks vanished when Satan attacked. Mrs. Job lost her status as the admired "leading lady" of her community.

Fourth, *she had lost her companion.* No more intimate moments with her husband. No more romantic conversations in front of a roaring fire. No more long walks together in the evenings, watching the desert sky ablaze with the dazzling colors of God's palette. Not only that, Job's wife had no indication that his situation would ever improve. So, either out of her bitterness toward God for allowing Job's suffering or her desire for her husband's misery to end, she advised Job to "take the easy way out" by cursing God and giving up on life.

Responding to Others' Pain

Though we sympathize with the agony of Job's wife, we can also see that her negative responses and poor advice only served to further alienate and discourage her husband. From her example, we discover what to do and what *not* to do when one of our own loved ones faces a difficult and painful situation.

First, *always guard your words when your loved one is going through a hard time.* Instead of shaming or blaming, offer a listening ear and kind words. During difficult times, your loved one needs a gentle dose of spiritual wisdom, perspective, and strength. Encourage your friend or family member and lift him or her up in prayer. And remember that actions speak louder than words. Find tangible ways to help. For example: Call to offer support, take a friend out for the evening, make dinner, baby-sit, share a ride, mow your friend's lawn, be there for an important ceremony, or send an encouraging card or gift to let your loved one know you care.

List one or more people in your life who seem to need encouragement right now.

How can you help minister to the needs of these individuals? List at least one tangible, encouraging gesture you could offer to each person on your list. Then write down a specific day or time when you will perform this gesture, and do it!

Next, *never suggest that your loved one should compromise his or her integrity.* Even though you may not understand why he or she is suffering, you're responsible to encourage your loved one to move *toward* God, not away from Him. Compromise may seem to offer temporary relief, but in the long run, it only makes the situation worse by allowing sin to widen the gap between your loved one and the Father. Offer a lifeline to your friend or family member by providing him or her with positive encouragement and creative reminders of God's love. Demonstrate to him or her that a strong faith in God is vital to achieving peace and restoration.

Think back to a time when a friend or family member helped you through a difficult time. What were the circumstances? What did the person say or do that encouraged you?

Job's Godly Responses

Though Job's wife offered him unwise advice, he maintained a godly response to her as well as to his traumatic situation. First, *he offered a godly response to his wife.* When Job's wife urged him to forget his integrity, curse God, and die, he told her, "You speak as one of the foolish women speaks" (Job 2:10).

Getting to the Root
The Hebrew word *nabal* used here means "spiritually ignorant or nondiscerning."[8] Instead of taking his wife's poor advice, Job gently reproved her for it, reminding her that God was still in control of his situation.

Second, *Job offered a godly response to his condition.* He asked his wife, "Shall we indeed accept good from the hand of God and not accept adversity?" (Job 2:10). Even in his suffering, Job had faith that God saw the big picture. Job knew that his circumstances weren't outside the realm of God's sovereignty or control. He also recognized that only by remaining faithful could he hold onto his spiritual peace and hope for restoration.

NUGGETS OF WISDOM

From Job's godly response and his wife's not-so-godly one, we can glean three truths to apply to our own lives.

First, *our lives are full of trials, and we need to remember that there are always more to come.* The difficult situation you may be facing isn't the first you've encountered, and it probably won't be the last, either. Job himself says in 5:7, "For man is born for trouble, as sparks fly upward." Trials represent an inevitable fact of life on earth, so don't be surprised when they come your way.

What is the most difficult trial you're currently facing? What have you learned from Job's godly response to adversity that you can apply to your own situation?

Second, *our world is fallen, and we need to understand that there are those who love us but will give us wrong advice.* We've all received poor advice at one time or another. Unfortunately, misguided advice can come from believers as well as from nonbelievers. You may hear it from your spouse, parents, children, other family members, friends, church members, neighbors, classmates, or colleagues. Be sure to consider each person's words carefully, and remember that guidance from others never replaces wisdom from God. Seek Him first regarding issues in your life, and filter everything you hear, say, and do through the grid of Scripture. The Bible, our standard, is the inspired Word of God. If you receive advice that contradicts Scripture, then you know that you shouldn't follow it.

Has a well-meaning friend or family member ever given you poor advice? If so, what was the situation? Did you take his or her advice? Why or why not?

Third, *since our God is sovereign, we must prepare ourselves for both blessing and adversity.* Life may be unfair and completely unpredictable, but God is sovereign. Sometimes He sends blessings; at others, He allows trials. But always, He has a purpose too great for us to fathom.

How can you prepare yourself for the trials that will inevitably come in your life?

How can you seek out God's blessings and prepare yourself to receive them?

The next time tests come your way, keep in mind that God sees the front of the beautiful, cosmic tapestry of His creation—including our lives—in gloriously full color, with every stitch perfectly planned and executed. In contrast, from our limited viewpoint, we see only the maze of knots and seemingly aimless threads on the underside of that tapestry. One day, we'll see the tapestry from our heavenly vantage point and view the completed work of God's hand. Until then, we're called to trust His heart.

4 Job's Advice to Friends and Husbands

Job 2:11–13

> Then they sat down on the ground with him for seven days and seven nights with no one speaking a word to him, for they saw that his pain was very great.
>
> —Job 2:13

IF CHRISTOPHER COLUMBUS had turned back before reaching the Americas, no one would have blamed him, but no one would have remembered him, either! Similarly, if Job hadn't been able to withstand such monumental trials, we wouldn't have blamed him, but we also wouldn't remember him as a giant in the faith.

Thankfully, Job's patient endurance earned him a prominent place in the most important of history books—the Bible. Scripture applauds Job as a paragon of trust for remaining faithful despite the scorching heat of his crucible of trials.

The dictionary defines *crucible* as "a vessel of a very refractory material (as porcelain) used for melting and calcining a substance that requires a high degree of heat." Figuratively, *crucible* means "a place or situation in which concentrated forces interact to cause or influence change or development" or, more simply, "a severe test."[1] Job certainly experienced more than his share of severe tests! He needed his friends and loved ones to surround him with understanding and compassion. But sadly, that didn't happen.

As we explore the responses of Job's friends and family to his tragedy, we'll learn what to say to those who are suffering, as well as when to remain silent. We'll also gain tools for encouraging our loved ones to emerge as refined gold from the crucibles of their trials.

TREASURES FROM THE TEXT

Response from an Angry Wife

Remember the misguided advice that Job's wife offered him earlier in chapter 2: "Do you still hold fast your integrity? Curse God and die!" (Job 2:9).

His wife's angry, biting words stung Job's heart like lemon juice poured in an open wound. Yet he still managed to respond to her with a kind, gentle reproof: "'You speak as one of the foolish women speaks. Shall we indeed accept good from God and not accept adversity?' In all this Job did not sin with his lips" (Job 2:10).

Response from Job's Friends

No doubt, the news of Job's distress had spread faster than a speeding camel throughout his community. When three of Job's friends heard of his predicament, they rushed to the scene . . . and couldn't believe their eyes.

> Now when Job's three friends heard of all this adversity that had come upon him, they came each one from his own place, Eliphaz the Temanite, Bildad the Shuhite and Zophar the Naamathite; and they made an appointment together to come to sympathize with him and comfort him. (Job 2:11)

Why did Job's friends come to see him, according to this passage?

Do you think Job's friends might have had other reasons for coming to see him as well? If so, what might they have been?

What is normally your first response when a sudden, painful situation occurs in the life of a friend or family member?

Why do you think you respond this way?

> When they lifted up their eyes at a distance and did not recognize him, they raised their voices and wept. And each of them tore his robe and they threw dust over their heads toward the sky. (Job 2:12)

Job's friends expressed their grief and despair in three ways. First, they wept aloud, indicating their emotional shock and sorrow. Second, they tore their robes to signify their broken-heartedness. Job had responded in a similar fashion when he heard of the deaths of his children. Third, Job's friends threw dust on their heads to symbolize their deep grief (also see 1 Samuel 4:12; 2 Samuel 1:2; and Nehemiah 9:1).[2]

Compare the response of Job's three friends with Job's own response to his calamity in 1:20. How are the responses similar? How are they different?

After coming to see Job, his three friends did a most unusual thing to help comfort him in his affliction:

> Then they sat down on the ground with him for seven days and seven nights with no one speaking a word to him, for they saw that his pain was very great. (Job 2:13)

Clearly, Job's friends held Job in high regard. They perceived the extreme depth of his grief and despair, and out of respect for his suffering, they sacrificed their own needs to stay with him for seven days and nights. Bible scholar Dr. Roy Zuck offers this insight regarding the response of Job's friends:

> Sitting down in silence with him for a week may have been their way of mourning over his deathlike condition, or it may have been an act of sympathy and comfort, or a reaction of horror. Whatever the reason, in the custom of that day they allowed the grieving person to express himself first.[3]

How do you think his friends' compassion and willingness to share in his grief ministered to Job?

What was significant about the three men's silence?

Have you ever been in a situation where "silence was the best medicine"? If so, what were the circumstances?

In Other Words

The quiet companionship and comfort initially offered by his friends must have brought Job great relief and encouragement. But once the three men opened their mouths to offer Job some "spiritual" advice, their compassionate ministry abruptly ended.

In the following chapters of this study guide, we'll explore the verbal responses of Job's friends. The sting of their sharp accusations and hurtful words will shock you! But before we delve into the speeches of these three men, take a moment to read Eugene Peterson's astute assessment of Job's friends and their not-so-good advice:

> There is more to the book of Job than Job. There are Job's friends. The moment we find ourselves in trouble of any kind—sick in the hospital, bereaved by a friend's death, dismissed from a job or relationship, depressed or bewildered—people start showing up telling us exactly what is wrong with us and what we must do to get better. Sufferers attract fixers the way roadkills attract vultures. At first we are impressed that they bother with us and amazed at their facility with answers. They know so much! How did they get to be such experts in living?
>
> More often than not, these people use the Word of God frequently and loosely. They are full of spiritual diagnosis and prescription. It all sounds so hopeful. But then we begin to wonder, "Why is it that for all their apparent compassion we feel worse instead of better after they've said their piece?"
>
> . . . Many of the answers that Job's so-called friends give him are technically true. But it is the "technical" part that ruins them. They are answers without personal relationship, intellect without intimacy. The answers are slapped onto Job's ravaged life like labels on a specimen bottle. Job rages against this secularized wisdom that has lost touch with the living realities of God.[4]

When we're suffering, we don't need blame, shame, trite answers, or false labels. Instead, we need true friends. We seek out listening ears and open hearts. We desire comfort and companionship. In order to mend, our hurting spirits need a healing dose of compassion and encouragement.

When we experience suffering, we intuitively know what we need to help *us* through. Yet how often do we offer the same caring friendship, comfort, love, and support to *others* who suffer? Let's take this opportunity to evaluate our care and compassion levels as we learn how to respond to others' trials in a godly way.

Job's Advice for Comforting Others

From Job's response to his wife and friends, we can glean four principles for comforting others in their times of need.

First, listen well, and always tell others the truth. Most of us aren't hard of hearing; we're hard of listening. We tend to forget that God had a reason for giving each of us two ears and only one mouth! Often, listening is the best gift you can offer a struggling loved one. Focus on understanding his or her situation and empathizing with his or her pain before you attempt to say anything. If you do feel led to speak, offer a word of comfort and share the truth in love. Job modeled this by offering a godly response to his wife's bitter words and his friends' misguided advice.

On a scale of one to ten, with ten being the highest, how would you rate yourself as a listener? How do you think your spouse, family members, friends, and coworkers would rate you?

What can you do to improve your listening skills?

Second, *turn others toward God.* Job reminded his wife that the Lord is sovereign over every moment of our lives. Our Almighty God is never caught off guard by events or circumstances! Nothing happens that's beyond His knowledge or control. Job recognized that he and his wife were players in God's divine drama. As the curtain opened with a flourish and Job suddenly stumbled onto center stage, he had to trust that the Lord had scripted a plan far beyond his comprehension.

How do you attempt to turn others toward God in your daily life?

How would you describe your role in God's "divine drama"? How do your words, actions, and activities support your part in this drama?

Third, *model verbal purity.* Job 2:10 reads, "In all this Job did not sin with his lips." Job could have responded to his wife in anger and frustration. But rather, he provided her with a gentle reminder of God's blessing and provision. Instead of cursing God, as his wife encouraged him to do, Job blessed the name of the Lord.

In what areas do you need to improve your verbal purity? What steps can you take to do this?

Worship leader and musician Matt Redman echoes Job's godly response in his heart-probing worship song entitled "Blessed Be the Name":

> Blessed be Your name
> In the land that is plentiful
> Where Your streams of abundance flow
> Blessed be Your name.
>
> And blessed be Your name
> When I'm found in the desert place
> Though I walk through the wilderness
> Blessed be Your name.
>
> Every blessing you pour out
> I'll turn back to praise.
> And when the darkness closes in, Lord
> Still I will say
>
> Blessed be the name of the Lord
> Blessed be Your name.
> Blessed be the name of the Lord
> Blessed be Your glorious name.
>
> You give and take away
> You give and take away
> My heart will choose to say,
> Lord, blessed be Your name.[5]

Do these words reflect the cry of your heart right now? In what ways can you bless the Lord no matter what circumstances you face?

Fourth, *accept others completely and love them unconditionally.* We thrive in contexts where we're appreciated and loved for who we are, and yet are encouraged to become the people that God wants us to become. We form and cement our relationships with others by weaving cords of trust from thin, fragile threads. Each moment we spend together, each word, each shared experience or event, adds another thread to the cord. Each hurtful word or action destroys a thread, weakening the cord. We grow in our friendships and relationships with others by continually adding threads, thus strengthening our bonds with those we love.

Taking Truth to Heart

A note to husbands and wives here: Your spouse will thrive when you seek to provide a context of love and acceptance for him or her. You chose to spend the rest of your life with this man or woman, and the covenant you made before God binds you to this deeply committed relationship. You're in this marriage for better or worse, for richer or poorer, in sickness and in health.

When each of you places your faith in God and seeks the best for your mate, no amount of hardship will separate you. In fact, adversity will draw you closer to one another. When the crucible heats up, too many people look for ways to get out. Instead, when adversity strikes, find new ways to get connected! Take whatever steps are necessary to reconnect physically, spiritually, and emotionally with the love of your life. The health of your marriage depends on it.

Christian relationship experts Les and Leslie Parrott offer several tips for connecting with your mate. First, *take time to touch daily.* A gentle squeeze on your partner's shoulder as she's preparing a meal or a soft backrub as he's reading a book can communicate loving messages in ways our words never can.

Second, *laugh a lot together.* Laughter bonds people. It's like a vitamin supplement for your marriage. Proverbs 17:22 says, "A cheerful heart is good medicine." Don't take yourself so seriously. Laugh when you don't feel like laughing. Study your spouse's funny bone—find out what makes him or her laugh, and tap into that daily.

Third, *be encouraging.* Never underestimate the power of a positive spouse! When our mates boost our self-confidence, our options seem limitless. We all know we should try to avoid negative words, but we need more than just the absence of the negative; we require a regular diet of positive encouragement and uplifting words. Without them, our spirit—and our marriage—withers.[6]

If you're married, take a few minutes to assess your attitudes and actions toward your partner. Is God leading you to change the way you treat your mate? If so, what aspects of your life need to change?

Name one or two other people in your life who need acceptance and love. How can you demonstrate these qualities to them?

NUGGETS OF WISDOM

As we seek to support those we know who are hurting, let's examine five vital characteristics of a true friend.

Five Characteristics of a True Friend

1. *A true friend cares enough to respond without being invited to respond.* No one sent a message to Eliphaz, Bildad, and Zophar, saying, "Please come and give a little sympathy and comfort to Job. He's dying in his anguish." Instead, Job's friends just came. When your friends or family members go through a traumatic time, make an effort to call, stop by, send a card or letter, or somehow connect with them. Don't wait for an invitation to show that you care because a deeply hurting person will rarely offer one.

2. *A true friend responds with sympathy and comfort.* Friends identify with those who suffer. They comfort others by helping to make their sorrow lighter. They do what needs to be done: taking a loved one out to dinner, running errands, taking care of the kids, cooking a meal. Why? Because true friends have a covenant-type relationship that cannot be easily broken. And part of the covenant is the commitment to be there, no matter what. Your presence during the fun times will be remembered, but your presence during a crisis will be cherished even more.

3. *A true friend openly expresses the depth of his or her feelings.* When a true friend perceives a loved one's suffering, it's not uncommon to see him or her fighting back tears. Acquaintances don't do that, but friends do. They empathize with others' pain. When their loved ones suffer, they suffer. And when their loved ones celebrate, they celebrate.

4. *A true friend isn't turned off by distasteful sights.* Can you imagine how Job's friends must have felt when they saw Job for the first time after his disaster? He sat on a heap of ashes with his head shaven and his robe torn, his skin blackened and covered with hideous boils. An acrid cloud of smoke rose from the burning piles of animal dung that surrounded him. Ravenous dogs roamed through the rubbish, searching for scraps of food. Some of the dogs even stopped to lick Job's sores. Unthinkable!

No doubt, Job's friends were stunned beyond belief at this sight. Yet they stuck by him. They expressed their grief outwardly and then sat down to mourn with their friend for seven days and seven nights. They exposed themselves to the ashes, dogs, waste, and outcasts in order to show Job that they cared. Now, that's commitment!

5. *A true friend understands and has to say very little.* Compassion, not judgment, heals hearts. We offer more comfort to hurting souls when we listen than when we try to explain everything. A caring hug, a warm squeeze of the hand, a visit to a hospital room, a heartfelt prayer . . . these are what friends offer in tough times.

Of these five characteristics of a true friend, which are you best at modeling?

Which of these characteristics do you need to cultivate more in your life? How can you improve your response in these areas?

No doubt, studying these characteristics of a true friend has brought to your mind several friends or family members who need your encouragement right now. Maybe your beloved mother has cancer, she's lost all of her hair as a result of her chemotherapy, and she weighs half of what she used to. Perhaps your father can't take care of himself anymore, and you've had to make the difficult decision to place him in a nursing home. Maybe your sister's husband walked out on her, or your brother's battling a drug or alcohol problem. Perhaps a friend's child recently passed away in a car accident.

How can you apply the five principles of friendship to your relationships with suffering friends, family members, or coworkers?

Keep in mind that your presence means the world to a suffering person. Even if you don't know exactly what to say, *be there.* Your compassion and care will make an eternal difference in the life of your loved one!

5 The Mournful Wail of a Miserable Man

Selections from Job 3

> ## Let the day perish on which I was to be born.
>
> ### —Job 3:3

GREAT PEOPLE often have humble beginnings.

The renowned Austrian composer Gustav Mahler lived a life marked by tragedy. During his early years, he lost seven brothers and sisters. According to one author, "The coffin became a regular piece of furniture in [the Mahler] house."[1] In addition, Mahler was raised in an abusive home. Mahler's father, a cruel alcoholic, often took out his rage on his wife—a vulnerable invalid who was at the mercy of her husband's blows.

Mahler eventually married, and he and his wife had a lovely daughter whom he adored. Mahler loved nature and the outdoors, and he had a magnificent laugh and an infectious love of life. His family enjoyed good times together. But his beloved daughter died at age four, and Mahler never truly recovered from the loss. In addition, authorities forced the composer to quit his work at the Vienna Opera House because of his Jewish heritage. Shortly afterward, his doctors informed him that he had a heart condition and wouldn't live much longer.

But, amazingly, in the midst of all this turmoil, Gustav Mahler composed his magnificent Ninth Symphony, one of classical music's best-loved, richest, and most complex creations.

By doing so, he transformed his painful past into something priceless and beautiful. He didn't forget his hardships; instead, he wove them into the musical tapestry of his art. The lessons he learned and the trials he endured became as much a part of his music as the laughter and special moments he shared with his wife and daughter.

In the same way, the book of Job has ministered to the hurting for centuries because Job truly *understood* suffering. It's no surprise that those who experience times of grief and depression turn to Job for strength, since only those with wounded hearts can truly empathize with such deep and tortured anguish.

Treasures from the Text

Job's heartrending lament begins in chapter 3, recorded in poetic form rather than in narrative prose. The meter and descriptive language of Hebrew poetry provide a powerful, metaphoric means for Job to unleash his deep-seated emotions of pain, despair, and loneliness.

Job's Lament

> Job opened his mouth and cursed the day of his birth.
> And Job said,
>> "Let the day perish on which I was to be born,
>> And the night which said, 'A boy is conceived.'
>> May that day be darkness;
>> Let not God above care for it,
>> Nor light shine on it.
>> Let darkness and black gloom claim it;
>> Let a cloud settle on it;
>> Let the blackness of the day terrify it." (Job 3:1–5)

After reading verse 1, we might tend to say, "Aha! Satan was right. Job did curse God." But he didn't. He cursed *the day of his birth*. There's a big difference! Asking "Why was I ever born?" isn't the same as saying, "I no longer believe in you, God." Job's outburst wasn't prompted only by his physical suffering, but also by the fact that he felt out of touch with God. He felt so alone that he regretted ever drawing his first breath, and he wished he could erase the day of his birth.

Have you ever felt a deep sense of loneliness or isolation? If so, what were the circumstances?

What helped you make it through these experiences?

What did you learn about God and about yourself through these difficult times?

Job continued in Job 3:6–10:

> As for that night, let darkness seize it;
> Let it not rejoice among the days of the year;
> Let it not come into the number of the months.
> Behold, let that night be barren;
> Let no joyful shout enter it.
> Let those curse it who curse the day. . . .
> Let the stars of its twilight be darkened;
> Let it wait for light but have none,
> And let it not see the breaking dawn;
> Because it did not shut the opening of my mother's womb,
> Or hide trouble from my eyes.

Which images in verses 1–10 reveal to you the depth of Job's emotions?

Job regretted his birth and even his conception (Job 3:1–10). He wished he had been still-born (3:11–19), and he longed to die (3:20–26). He wished that the sun had never come up on the day he was born, and he longed for God to reverse the order of His creative act described in Genesis 1:3. He begged God to "let there be darkness" instead of light on the day of his birth. One author writes, "Death is for him now sweeter than life, and he pictures the pleasures of [the afterlife] compared to his present lot" (see Job 3:13, 17).[2]

Wait a minute, you might be thinking. This is too unfair! How could a godly man like Job be put in a position like this, wishing that he had never been born? What about all the people who told us that if we walk closely with God, we'll live happily ever after? What about the promise that God loves us and has a wonderful plan for our lives?

Job jolts us back to reality—God's reality. God's plan for His creation *is* wonderful, so wonderful that we cannot comprehend it. But our frame of reference is different from His. A situation that may seem horrible to us at the time might be God's way of working for our greater good and for the glory of His creation. Not only does God promise us that He will work things out for *His* good, but He also promises us that He will work them out for *our* good (Romans 8:28). And that's great news! We cling to the hope that somehow, some way, someday, God is going to make something good from Job's situation—and ours.

Windows to the Ancient World

In the ancient Near East, family and friends customarily shouted with joy and congratulations when a son was born, since he would be an asset to his family and an heir to his parents' estate. In contrast, Job said in Job 3:7, "Let that night be barren; Let no joyful shout enter it." He would have preferred silence to the shouts of joy on the day of his birth.

In verse 8, Job referred to an ancient myth suggesting that certain enchanters could make a day unfortunate (curse it) by raising Leviathan (see Job 41:1; Psalm 74:14; 104:26; Isaiah 27:1). The term "Leviathan" represented a seven-headed sea monster of ancient Near Eastern mythology. It was believed that, when awakened, this sea beast could cause an eclipse by swallowing the sun or the moon. Job suggests in poetic terms that if Leviathan had swallowed the sun or the moon on that day, then his birthday would, in a sense, not exist at all.[3]

In *The Message,* Eugene Peterson offers this poignant rendering of Job 3:1–10:

> Obliterate the day I was born.
>> Blank out the night I was conceived!
> Let it be a black hole in space.
>> May God above forget it ever happened.
>> Erase it from the books!
> May the day of my birth be buried in deep darkness,
>> shrouded by the fog,
>> swallowed by the night.
> And the night of my conception—the devil take it!
>> Rip the date off the calendar,
>> delete it from the almanac.
> Oh, turn that night into pure nothingness—
>> no sounds of pleasure from that night, ever!
> May those who are good at cursing curse that day.
>> Unleash the sea beast, Leviathan, on it.
> May its morning stars turn to black cinders,
>> waiting for a daylight that never comes,
>> never once seeing the first light of dawn.
> And why? Because it released me from my mother's womb
>> into a life with so much trouble. (MSG)

What fresh insights into this passage can you glean from Peterson's interpretation of these verses?

In Job 3:11–26, Job continued his lament by asking a series of rhetorical questions. In verses 11 through 19, he asked, "Why was I ever born?" One author notes, "Having been born dead would have been better than his present existence of turmoil."[4] Job asserted that if he had been stillborn, he could have slept in peace in his grave along with past kings, princes, and counselors of the earth. But instead, he was forced to live in utter anguish.

The question "Why did the knees receive me?" (Job 3:12) most likely refers either to Job's mother's giving birth and taking her son in her lap soon afterward, or to the ancient custom of placing a newborn child on the knees of his father or a paternal ancestor to indicate that the child was accepted as legitimate (see Genesis 50:23).[5]

In Job 3:20–26, Job's anguish reached a climax. Since he had already been conceived and born, and since he hadn't been stillborn, he longed for death to come now to end his suffering. He communicated the crux of his pain in verses 25 and 26: "For what I fear comes upon me, and what I dread befalls me. I am not at ease, nor am I quiet, and I am not at rest, but turmoil comes."

Five times in this chapter, Job asked God "why?" List the verses where this question appears.

What might it say about Job that he posed this question repeatedly to God?

In which areas of your life would you like to ask God "why?"

How does it stretch your faith when you experience situations that you can't predict or control?

Charles Haddon Spurgeon, the popular nineteenth-century British pastor, experienced feelings of inadequacy, depression, despair, and disillusionment that mirrored Job's in some ways. In a lecture to his students called "The Minister's Fainting Fits," Spurgeon stated openly:

Before any great achievement, some measure of the same depression is very usual. . . . Such was my experience when I first became a pastor in London. My success appalled me; and the thought of the career which it seemed to open up, so far from elating me, cast me into the lowest depths, out of which I uttered my *miserere* and found no room for a *gloria in excelsis*. Who was I that I should continue to lead so great a multitude? I would betake me to my village obscurity, or emigrate to America and find a solitary nest in the backwoods, where I might be sufficient for the things which would be demanded of me. . . . This depression comes over me whenever the Lord is preparing a larger blessing for my ministry; the cloud is black before it breaks, and overshadows before it yields its deluge of mercy. Depression has now become to me as a prophet in rough clothing.[6]

We've all struggled at times with feelings of painful inadequacy, depression, or utter insufficiency to complete a task or bear a load. When we travel through these dark, rocky valleys, many of us tend to isolate ourselves from others. Job, however, didn't run and hide. He didn't "stuff" his emotions or try to downplay his pain. He openly unleashed his grief and cried out to God. He wasn't afraid to wrestle with God in his attempt to come to terms with the tough trials that plagued him.

In Other Words

Phillip Yancey writes,

Very often, disappointment with God begins in Job-like circumstances. The death of a child, a tragic accident, or a loss of job may bring on the same questions Job asked. Why me? What does God have against me? Why does he seem so distant? . . .

For Job, the battleground of faith involved lost possessions, lost family members, lost health. We may face a different struggle: a career failure, a floundering marriage, sexual orientation, a body shape that turns people off, not on. At such times the outer circumstances—the illness, the bank account, the run of bad luck—will seem the real struggle. We may beg God to change those circumstances. *If only I were beautiful or handsome, then everything would work out. If only I had more money—or at least a job—then I could easily believe God.*

But the more important battle, as shown in Job, takes place inside us. Will we trust God? Job teaches that at the moment when faith is hardest and *least* likely, then faith is most needed.[7]

Describe your "battleground of faith." What battles are you currently fighting?

What steps can you take to keep your faith strong while you fight these battles?

NUGGETS OF WISDOM

Chapter 3 of Job is difficult for us to read because it illustrates Job's anguish during his darkest period of suffering. We have a tough time swallowing the bitter medicine that Job was forced to take. But we've all experienced despair, and we've all had friends who have been hit by tragedy. We need to know what to do when our loved ones face monumental trials. We need to know where to find hope when the heavens seem hopelessly silent. From Job's lament, we can glean three principles to apply to our daily lives.

First of all, *some days are too dark for the sufferer to see light.* Those who have lost a spouse, friend, or family member through death or divorce will tell you that, even years after the tragedy, they have good days and bad days. On the good days, the pain seems manageable. On the bad days, it's almost unbearable. But guess what? God can handle even your bad days. He knows your hurts. And there's nothing you can say to Him that He hasn't heard before!

Don't you appreciate the transparency Job demonstrated in his lament? He blurted out exactly how he felt. He informed God and the world that he wished he had never been born at all. The pain, the suffering, and the grief were one thing to deal with, but God's silence was quite another. Yet Job found a way to express himself while maintaining his integrity and his faith in God.

If you were to write a lament right now, what issues and desires would you present to the Lord?

Second, *some experiences are too extreme for the hurting to find hope.* Did Job hope that he would be restored? Probably. Yet from his outcries, it seems that he never truly expected to be healed. Amazingly, he never even asked for healing! What he asked for were answers from Yahweh and a reprieve from His deafening silence.

It took some time for Job to gain perspective on his suffering. Yet he believed deep in his heart that God had some reason for allowing this calamity. He maintained faith that the Lord was somehow still sovereign over his suffering.

How does your life show that God is sovereign, even in the midst of your trials?

Third, *some valleys are too deep for the anguished to find relief.* Grief and depression are natural responses to life in a fallen world. If you're struggling through the grieving process or suffering from depression, don't blame yourself. Everyone walks through valleys of despair, and everyone feels burdened at one time or another by the tremendous weight of their trials. *Having a godly response* to those trials is what matters most.

You may be experiencing symptoms of grief or depression. These could include extreme sadness, despair, anger, sleeplessness, exhaustion, lack of energy or motivation, or inability to perform everyday tasks. If you're suffering from these symptoms, please seek help from a trusted Christian counselor. Insight for Living has caring, experienced pastors and licensed counselors available to help you deal with difficult issues. Simply call our Pastoral Care Line at (972) 473-5097. You may also access our Web site at www.insight.org to download ministry tools, information, useful links, and answers to your questions on a wide array of practical topics.

God's Promise to Those Who Suffer

It's okay to admit that we don't always understand the principles and purposes behind our trials. God can handle our grievances! He loves us, and He wants to bring us to greater maturity through our painful experiences. The prophet Isaiah tells us that our Father sent His Son

> To bring good news to the afflicted;
> . . . to bind up the brokenhearted,
> To proclaim liberty to captives
> And freedom to prisoners; . . .
> Giving them a garland instead of ashes,
> The oil of gladness instead of mourning,
> The mantle of praise instead of a spirit of fainting.
> So they will be called oaks of righteousness,
> The planting of the LORD, that He may be glorified.
> (Isaiah 61:1, 3; see also Luke 4:18–19)

God can heal even the most painful broken heart. Keep trusting Him through your trials, and He'll exchange your ashes of mourning for the beauty of joy and praise.

6 Responding to Bad Counsel

Selections from Job 4–7

> I rejoice in unsparing pain,
> That I have not denied the words of the Holy One.
> —Job 6:10

NOT ALL ADVICE IS GOOD ADVICE.

When you were a teenager, someone may have told you, "You're bright and talented. Why even bother going to college? Plenty of people have become millionaires who never even finished high school!" Or perhaps your best friend advised you, "Oh, go ahead and get married. It'll work out. He'll change!" Or maybe when you started investing a few years ago, your stockbroker said, "I have a good feeling about this. I think you'd be wise to invest $10,000 in Enron stock." Not a good plan!

Unfortunately, those who give bad counsel often think it's good counsel. In fact, the greater part of the book of Job contains speeches from men who thought they were offering Job wise advice. They sincerely believed that they were helping their suffering friend. But not only were these men wrong, their unkind words only served to deepen Job's pain. They completely lost sight of their original purpose—"to sympathize with him and comfort him" (Job 2:11).

After Job broke his week-long silence with an outcry of bitter anguish, his three friends Eliphaz, Bildad, and Zophar felt compelled to speak. Each one shared his advice and was then answered by Job. This cycle occurred three times, with one variation in the third round: Zophar did not speak again.

Job's friends addressed him from different perspectives: Eliphaz, from experience (see Job 4:8; 5:3; 15:17); Bildad, from tradition (see 8:8); and Zophar, from his own assumptions (see 11:13–15). Throughout their speeches, these three men maintained the faulty theological position that the righteous are always rewarded and the unrighteous are always punished.

They suggested that to be experiencing such agony, Job must have willfully sinned and therefore needed to repent.

The reasoning of Job's friends followed a *syllogism,* "a deductive scheme of a formal argument consisting of a major and a minor premise and a conclusion."[1] They suggested that all suffering is punishment for sin (major premise); Job is suffering (minor premise); therefore, Job must have committed sin (conclusion). But this directly contradicted God's statement that Job was "blameless and upright" (see 1:1; 2:3).

TREASURES FROM THE TEXT

Eliphaz's Speech

Job 4 and 5 record Eliphaz's first speech, in which he asserts that since the innocent do not suffer, Job must not be innocent.

> Then Eliphaz the Temanite answered,
> "If one ventures a word with you, will you become impatient?
> But who can refrain from speaking?
> Behold you have admonished many,
> And you have strengthened weak hands.
> Your words have helped the tottering to stand,
> And you have strengthened feeble knees.
> But now it has come to you, and you are impatient;
> It touches you, and you are dismayed.
> Is not your fear of God your confidence,
> And the integrity of your ways your hope?" (Job 4:1–6)

What compliments did Eliphaz pay Job in this passage?

What accusations did Eliphaz make against Job? How were they misguided?

Eliphaz continued to let the arrows fly:

> Remember now, who ever perished being innocent?
> Or where were the upright destroyed?
> According to what I have seen, those who plow iniquity
> And those who sow trouble harvest it. . . .
> For man is born for trouble,
> As sparks fly upward.
> But as for me, I would seek God,
> And I would place my cause before God. (Job 4:7–8; 5:7–8)

In Other Words

Not only did Eliphaz accuse Job of sin, he pridefully suggested what *he* would do if he were in Job's place. Eugene Peterson offers this pointed paraphrase:

> Would you mind if I said something to you?
>   Under the circumstances it's hard to keep quiet.
> You yourself have done this plenty of times, spoken words
>   that clarify, encouraged those who were about to quit.
> Your words have put stumbling people on their feet,
>   put fresh hope in people about to collapse.
> But now *you're* the one in trouble—you're hurting!
>   You've been hit hard and you're reeling from the blow.
> But shouldn't your devout life give you confidence now?
>   Shouldn't your exemplary life give you hope?
> Think! Has a truly innocent person ever ended up on the scrap heap?
>   Do genuinely upright people ever lose out in the end?
> It's my observation that those who plow evil
>   and sow trouble reap evil and trouble." (Job 4:2–8 MSG, emphasis added)

Essentially, Eliphaz accused Job of not being able to take his own advice. Job had encouraged and uplifted others who suffered, yet he felt discouraged by his own suffering. Job desperately needed the support of his friend, yet Eliphaz offered him nothing but criticism, taunts, and accusations of impiety.

Chapters 6 and 7 contain Job's response to Eliphaz's condemning speech. Job cried out in utter despair at the hurtful words of his friend. Yet he still maintained his innocence. He declared,

> Oh that my request might come to pass,
> And that God would grant my longing!
> Would that God were willing to crush me,
> That He would loose His hand and cut me off!
> But it is still my consolation,
> And I rejoice in unsparing pain,
> That I have not denied the words of the Holy One. (Job 6:8–10)

Job's only consolation was the knowledge that he had not defied God. This is the first of several of Job's affirmations of his innocence (see also Job 9:21; 16:17; 27:6).

Taking Truth to Heart

Before we explore the bad counsel given by Eliphaz, let's explore some passages from the book of Proverbs that illustrate the importance and characteristics of good counsel:

> The way of a fool is right in his own eyes,
> But a wise man is he who listens to counsel. (Proverbs 12:15)

> Pleasant words are a honeycomb,
> Sweet to the soul and healing to the bones. (Proverbs 16:24)

> Like apples of gold in settings of silver
> Is a word spoken in right circumstances. (Proverbs 25:11)

> Iron sharpens iron,
> So one man sharpens another. (Proverbs 27:17)

We've all known the benefit of a good friend who "sharpens" us with his or her wise counsel. Solomon expresses a similar thought later in chapter 27:

> As in water face reflects face,
> So the heart of man reflects man. (Proverbs 27:19)

No doubt, you've known occasions when another person's heart reflected your own concerns and desires. Perhaps you had a deep sorrow or concern in the well of your heart that you struggled to pull up. Then along came someone you loved and trusted who could drop a bucket into that deep well, pull out your sorrow, and comfort and encourage you.

On the other hand, sometimes love prompts our friends to give us counsel that isn't easy for us to hear: "Faithful are the wounds of a friend, but deceitful are the kisses of an enemy" (Proverbs 27:6).

The Hebrew language that Solomon uses in the first half of the verse suggests this literal translation: "Faithful are the wounds *caused by* the one who loves you." Sometimes we receive emotional or spiritual "bruises" from the words of those who genuinely love us and want to encourage us to grow. These bruises from friends stay with us for a long time, but usually, if they've been offered in love and with discretion, we're the better for having received them. Such faithful bruising helps us more in our walk with God than false flattery, trite remarks, or a phony embrace from someone who has their own best interests, not ours, at heart.

An effective word of exhortation, however, must be presented with a loving spirit and at the right time. When we're hurting deeply, we don't need additional wounds from friends. We depend on them to provide love, comfort, encouragement, and wisdom during challenging times. Positive words spoken from a loving heart in the right circumstances may be just the ray of sunlight we need to break through the clouds on a dark, depressing, lonely day.

What's the best advice you've ever gotten? What made it so wise?

On whom do you depend for counsel in difficult situations, and why?

Lessons Learned from Eliphaz's Poor Advice

First, *assumptions reduce understanding and insight.* Instead of responding to Job's suffering with comfort and compassion, Eliphaz started preaching. He assumed that Job had committed sin, and that God had sent trouble upon Job as direct punishment for that sin. But, as scholar Roy Zuck notes: "Such a theory . . . simply does not fit all the facts. Many times the innocent *do* suffer . . . and often the wicked seemingly have no problems. This was Job's point throughout the book; Eliphaz's view of an airtight doctrine of retribution does not jibe with reality."[3]

We must be careful what we assume about others' painful situations, and encourage rather than blame them. Much of the suffering in life happens simply as a result of the Fall (when sin entered the world through Adam), not because of the sufferer's own sin. Even when we do reap the consequences of our poor choices and sinful actions, positive words encourage life change much more powerfully than shame and blame.

If you had been in Job's place, what could Eliphaz have said and done to encourage you?

Is anyone in your life struggling through a Job-sized problem right now? If so, how can you show your friendship and support for him or her?

Second, *shame blocks grace and hinders relief and recovery.* What's the difference between guilt and shame? Christian author and counselor Jeff VanVonderan hits it right on the head:

> Shame is often confused with guilt. But they're not the same. God created you and me so that when we do something wrong we experience a sense of guilt. Guilt is like a spiritual nerve-response to sin, an emotion in response to wrong *behavior.* . . . In that sense, guilt is a healthy thing. Because guilt comes as a result of something you and I *do,* we can do something about it. . . .
>
> Shame, on the other hand, . . . is the belief or mindset that something is wrong with *you.* . . . It's not that you feel bad about your behavior, it's that you sense or believe *you* are deficient, defective or worthless as a human being.[4] (emphasis added)

Shame is not from God; it's from Satan. Our Father never shames us. Instead, He forgives and redeems us as His children, whom He loves. The devil, however, uses shame to make us feel unworthy. He wants to drain our joy and peace in Christ and poison our relationships with those we love. Through shame, he wants to make sure that we don't accept God's forgiveness, move past our mistakes and sins, and actively pursue God's will for our lives. Shame-based counsel like that offered by Job's friends loads us down with disgrace rather than lightening our burden with grace. Shame pushes us further into the downward spiral of our pain.

Name a situation in your life that brought you shame. What did other people do that either helped free you from that shame or burdened you with more shame? If the latter, how did you work through that issue?

Third, we learn from Eliphaz that *pride eclipses mercy and compassion.* Eliphaz, Bildad, and Zophar pridefully thought they had all the answers to Job's problems. Instead of offering listening ears and compassionate hearts, they heaped condemnation and blame on Job. Instead of mercifully caring for their suffering friend, they tried to "fix" him. They couldn't bear to admit that they didn't understand the mysteries of God's ways. As a result, they multiplied Job's pain instead of soothing it.

How have you experienced mercy and compassion from someone when you were hurting?

What impact did this person's kindness have on you?

NUGGETS OF WISDOM

Lessons Learned from Job's Response

We can glean two vital life lessons from Job's response to Eliphaz. First, *sometimes others' poor advice only makes our troubles worse.* When we're suffering, we don't need harsh words and misguided preaching. Instead, we long for the quiet presence of a friend. We appreciate kind words, a warm hug, and a shoulder to cry on. We're thankful for those who offer to provide meals, baby-sit, or help out with everyday chores in the face of an unexpected loss or hardship. To a suffering person, an action is worth a thousand words!

Can you think of a time when you preached or advised, but what was needed was simply compassion? If so, how effective was your preaching or advice?

Second, *sometimes trying to understand God's unfathomable ways only makes us more confused.* We don't understand the reasons behind everything that happens in our lives, and we aren't meant to. We seek to grow in our knowledge of God and His Word, but His ways are still too marvelous, too mysterious, and too great for us to fully fathom. That's why He's God!

If we had all the answers and knew every aspect of God's plan for our lives, we'd have no need for faith. And the Bible says, "Without faith it is impossible to please Him, for he who comes to God must believe that He is and that He is a rewarder of those who seek Him" (Hebrews 11:6). As Christians, our goal is to glorify and serve the Lord as we seek spiritual wisdom and maturity in a community of faith.

Read Hebrews 11. Who are the people listed in this "faith hall of fame"? List them on the left below. On the right, name some of the characteristics of these faithful people that stand out to you.

What do you find in Hebrews 11:35–38 that directly contradicts Eliphaz's argument that the godly do not suffer?

According to Hebrews 11:39–40, what hope do believers have regarding the suffering we experience on earth?

The next time you interact with a friend, family member, or even a stranger who is suffering, seek to comfort him or her using the biblical principles you've learned in this chapter. Proverbs 17:17 says, "A friend loves at *all* times . . ." (emphasis added). That means loving others not just in the good times, but in the difficult times as well.

7 Continuing the Verbal Fistfight

Selections from Job 8–10

> There is no umpire between us,
> Who may lay his hand upon us both.
>
> —Job 9:33

IN THEIR BOOK *The Sacred Romance,* Brent Curtis and John Eldredge write:

> If we will listen, a Sacred Romance calls to us through our heart every moment of our lives. It whispers to us on the wind, invites us through the laughter of good friends, reaches out to us through the touch of someone we love. We've heard it in our favorite music, sensed it at the birth of our first child, been drawn to it while watching the shimmer of a sunset on the ocean. The Romance is even present in times of great personal suffering: the illness of a child, the loss of a marriage, the death of a friend. Something calls to us through experiences like these and rouses an inconsolable longing deep within our heart, wakening in us a yearning for intimacy, beauty, and adventure. . . .
>
> However we may describe this deep desire, it is the most important thing about us, our heart of hearts, the passion of our life. And the voice that calls to us in this place is none other than the voice of God.[1]

While our Sacred Romance with our Father begins in a place of beauty and innocence, we soon recognize that our enemy, Satan, is constantly trying to destroy us by sending us a negative message—what Curtis and Eldredge call "the message of the arrows." Satan pulls back his powerful bow and lets his poisonous arrows of sin, jealousy, rejection, pain, and affliction fly straight into our hearts. Curtis and Eldredge continue:

There are only two things that pierce the human heart, wrote Simone Weil. One is beauty. The other is affliction. And while we wish there were only beauty in the world, each of us has known enough pain to raise serious doubts about the universe we live in. From very early in life we know another message, warning us that the Romance has an enemy.[2]

Job and God had once shared a special friendship characterized by closeness and overflowing blessing. But now the enemy was using whatever arrows he could to try to make Job's faith falter. That included discouraging words from Job's best friends.

TREASURES FROM THE TEXT

Job's heart had certainly been pierced by more than its share of arrows from Satan's quiver. He had already suffered intense grief and pain. Not only that, but his friend Eliphaz had rebuked him in chapter 4. And instead of offering Job comfort after this discouraging encounter, another of his friends, Bildad, was next in line to lambast Job.

Look Up!

Bildad's argument in Job 8 revolves around three subjects: the character of God (8:1–7); the wisdom of the past (8:8–10); and evidence from nature (8:11–22). First, he implored Job to *look up*. Bildad offered misguided personal insight into the character of God and the reasons for Job's suffering.

> Then Bildad the Shuhite answered,
>> "How long will you say these things,
>> And the words of your mouth be a mighty wind?
>> Does God pervert justice?
>> Or does the Almighty pervert what is right?
>> If your sons sinned against Him,
>> Then He delivered them into the power of their transgression.
>> If you would seek God
>> And implore the compassion of the Almighty,

> If you are pure and upright,
> Surely now He would rouse Himself for you
> And restore your righteous estate.
> Though your beginning was insignificant,
> Yet your end will increase greatly." (Job 8:1–7)

H. L. Mencken wrote, "For every complex problem, there is a solution that is simple, neat, and wrong."[3] Bildad offers a simplistic solution to an extraordinarily difficult problem. As a result, not only does he fail miserably to solve the problem, he piles more accusation and blame on Job instead of comfort.

How did Bildad characterize Job in his speech? What false accusations did he make?

How did Bildad characterize God? What were the weaknesses of his argument?

Look Back!

Next, Bildad implored Job to *look back.* He exhorted his friend to seek wisdom from the past:

> Please inquire of past generations,
> And consider the things searched out by their fathers.
> For we are only of yesterday and know nothing,
> Because our days on earth are as a shadow.
> Will they not teach you and tell you,
> And bring forth words from their minds? (Job 8:8–10)

Bildad, a traditionalist, told Job, in effect, "Because you know nothing compared to the great sages of the past, you need to learn some lessons from them. Because our lives are so brief, we need to draw what we can from their experiences." But Job's experience was personal, and the circumstances surrounding it were unique. Since no one had ever before been in Job's place, he had no point of reference for his suffering. Even the teachings of his forefathers in the faith offered no solutions for his particular dilemma. His only hope was to hold onto his faith in God more tightly than ever.

What have you learned about suffering from others' experiences?

What have you learned about suffering from your own experiences that you couldn't have learned from anyone else?

Look Around!

Finally, Bildad exhorted Job to examine the evidence offered by nature (Job 8:11–22). He used the example of the Egyptian papyrus plant to support his cause-and-effect theory about Job's suffering. He said, in essence, "Can a plant grow and flourish without water? Of course not. Without water to nourish the root system, the plant dies." In the same way, he suggested that Job had experienced severe affliction because he had committed wrongs and refused to confess his sin. Bildad implied that if Job would simply admit his guilt, God would restore his health, his family, and his fortunes. In Job 8:21, he promised Job that God "will yet fill your mouth with laughter and your lips with shouting." But because Job had no unconfessed sin in his life, Bildad's words only caused more pain and confusion. One author writes,

> It seems almost incredible that Bildad would reply so callously. There is not only steely indifference to Job's plight, but an arrogant certainty that Job's children got just what they deserved and that Job was well on his way to the same fate. The lesson we must learn is that there are such people in the world and that they do their heartless disservice to mankind under the guise of being the special friend of God.[4]

Have you ever received hurtful advice from a friend or acquaintance? If so, what were the circumstances, and how did this experience affect you?

What good advice and positive encouragement have you received recently from friends or family members?

How have your loved ones' words helped to further your spiritual growth?

In Other Words

We often fail to realize how much power lies in our words. A kindly spoken word can have surprisingly positive results, but a carelessly spoken, hurtful word can devastate a life. One author describes the difficult assault by Job's friends this way:

[Job] is wounded by their harshness, stung by their censures, exasperated by their reproaches, and driven into antagonism by their arguments. They are the professed advocates of religious obligation. They represent the cause of God, enforcing his claims on Job and justifying his ways with him, which they do in a spirit that repels him, with assumptions that experience does not sanction, and which his own inner consciousness falsifies. . . .

Here, then, are Job's three friends who . . . are busily engaged in letting fly their poisoned arrows. . . . And here is Job himself exposed without shield or buckler to their dangerous attacks.[5]

Job's Reply to Bildad

Finally, Job had felt the barbs of enough flaming arrows and heard enough hurtful words. In chapter 9, he silenced Bildad with his poignant, passionate response. Job's response to Bildad could be summarized in four questions.

1. *If I could stand before God, what would I say?* Job bemoaned that he couldn't bring his case to trial before the Lord. He longed for God's mercy, but God seemed to be against him. So Job answered,

> In truth I know that this is so;
> But how can a man be in the right before God?
> If one wished to dispute with Him,
> He could not answer Him once in a thousand times.
> Wise in heart and mighty in strength,
> Who has defied Him without harm? . . .
> How then can I answer Him,
> And choose my words before Him?
> For though I were right, I could not answer;
> I would have to implore the mercy of my judge.
> If I called and He answered me,
> I could not believe that He was listening to my voice.
> For He bruises me with a tempest
> And multiplies my wounds without cause. . . .
> If it is a matter of power, behold, He is the strong one!
> And if it is a matter of justice, who can summon Him? (Job 9:1–4, 14–17, 19)

2. *If I could declare my own innocence, what good would it do?* Job constantly asserted his innocence before God and sought for justice to be served. Yet he continued to suffer spiritually, emotionally, and physically. He cried out:

> Though I am righteous, my mouth will condemn me;
> Though I am guiltless, He will declare me guilty.
> I am guiltless;

I do not take notice of myself;
I despise my life. (Job 9:20–21)

3. *If I tried to be positive and cheerful, how would it help me?* He sought wisdom from his friends. He sought direction and mercy from God. He tried his best to maintain his faith and hope despite all odds. Yet he was blasted from every side by poor advice, blame, negativity, or worse, silence. He exclaimed:

Though I say, "I will forget my complaint,
I will leave off my sad countenance and be cheerful,"
I am afraid of all my pains,
I know that You will not acquit me. (Job 9:27–28)

4. *If only I had a mediator, I could have my needs represented, and the truth would be told.* In the following verses, Job mourned the fact that he had no "umpire" to serve as an arbitrator between himself and God:

For He is not a man as I am that I may answer Him,
That we may go to court together.
There is no umpire between us,
Who may lay his hand upon us both.
Let Him remove His rod from me,
And let not dread of Him terrify me.
Then I would speak and not fear Him;
But I am not like that in myself. (Job 9:32–35)

Since Job lived two thousand or more years before Christ, he had no one to argue his case before God. Job's cry would be ours as well if it weren't for the work of Jesus Christ, our merciful Mediator. Thankfully, Jesus serves as our go-between with the Father. Paul wrote in 1 Timothy 2:5–6: "For there is one God, and one mediator also between God and men, the man Christ Jesus, who gave Himself as a ransom for all, the testimony given at the proper time."

Job Cries Out to God

In Job 10, Job turned his attention from Bildad and began to address God directly. He asked God several penetrating questions.

Read through chapter 10 and summarize these questions in your own words.

How did Job compare man's nature and knowledge with God's sovereignty and wisdom?

There are many times in life when we don't know the answers and can't understand God's plan. God wants us to cast our cares on Him (1 Peter 5:7), to pour out our feelings and frustrations to Him as Job did.

What inhibits you from turning to God when you feel negative emotions?

How do you think the hurtful words of Eliphaz and Bildad influenced Job's mood and attitudes toward his suffering?

Nuggets of Wisdom

From the advice given by Job's friends, we've learned that *when misery breaks our spirit, philosophical words don't help us cope.* Instead of offering Job an encouraging word and a helping hand, Bildad launched hurtful accusations at his friend. Nothing Bildad said brought relief or strength to Job in his misery.

Oliver Wendell Holmes wrote, "Don't flatter yourself that friendship authorizes you to say disagreeable things to your intimates. The nearer you come into relation with a person, the more necessary do tact and courtesy become."[6]

Having a close friendship with someone doesn't mean that we have the license to say whatever we want to that person! Instead, we're called to take extra care to show love and compassion. Not only that, but we're called to love our enemies as well as our friends (Matthew 5:44). Author Henry James wrote: "Three things in human life are important. The first is to be kind. The second is to be kind. And the third is to be kind."[7]

A lesson in kindness would have done Bildad (and Job) a lot of good! Practicing kindness is good for us, too. "Be kind to one another, tender-hearted, forgiving each other . . ." Paul instructed (Ephesians 4:32).

Name someone in your life who could use a healing dose of kindness and encouragement right now. How can you offer tangible support to this person?

Next, we've learned that *when a mediator can't be found, futile searches won't give us hope.* If Job learned one positive lesson from his sufferings, it was that only God could truly be depended upon. Even when God was silent, Job trusted that He was there. Even when God's dealings seemed incomprehensible and mysterious, Job recognized His sovereignty. Though Satan buffeted Job, his wife urged him to curse God and die, and his friends condemned him, the patriarch of patience stood the test. Instead of searching for hope in all the wrong places, Job placed his faith in God.

To whom or what do you tend to cling to find hope in difficult times?

Have you ever been in a situation in which a mediator was present? If so, what was the situation? How did the person help the parties involved to reach a solution?

Have you been in a situation in which you wished you had a mediator, but didn't? If so, what happened as a result?

What does it mean to you personally that Christ is your Mediator?

When James commended Job for his patient endurance, he pointed out that the outcome of his struggle was a tribute to God's faithfulness and mercy (James 5:11). Along the same lines, James gives us this assurance: "Every good thing given and every perfect gift is from above, coming down from the Father of lights, with whom there is no variation or shifting shadow" (James 1:17). Every gift from the hand of God, whether it seems positive or painful, serves a purpose in our lives. Even when the darkness threatens to destroy us, God still reigns supreme. His light casts out all darkness—every bit—and His sword and shield provide us protection against the dangerous arrows of the evil one.

8 When Rebuke and Resistance Collide

Selections from Job 11–14

> O that you would be completely silent,
> And that [your silence] would become your wisdom!
>
> —Job 13:5

HAVE YOU EVER NOTICED that problems don't just go away by themselves? In fact, it often seems that the harder you try to solve them, the worse they get. They can multiply like roaches; if you ignore them and refuse to deal with them, they'll take over the whole house!

Job tried to tackle his proliferating problems, but as they multiplied, his friends' unkind words increased as well. Not a single sentence of sympathy or comfort fell from the lips of any of them. In almost every chapter of Job, we find accusation, blame, and shame. We hear self-righteous preaching, insults, and sarcasm. We notice finger-pointing, judgment, and condemnation, while comfort is nowhere to be found.

TREASURES FROM THE TEXT

Zophar's Accusations

After the speeches of Eliphaz and Bildad, Job barely had time to catch his breath before his friend Zophar stepped up and knocked the wind out of him once more. Job 11 records Zophar's tirade of accusations against Job. His basis for these accusations? Pure legalism. Zophar rigidly adhered to his own preset belief system, regardless of the facts of Job's situation.

First, *Zophar accused Job of being guilty of sin:*

> Then Zophar the Naamathite answered,
>   "Shall a multitude of words go unanswered,
>   And a talkative man be acquitted?
>   Shall your boasts silence men?
>   And shall you scoff and none rebuke?
>   For you have said, 'My teaching is pure,
>   And I am innocent in your eyes.'" (Job 11:1–4)

Because Zophar spoke last, we can assume he was probably the youngest of the three friends. His first speech was short and concise, but what it lacked in length, it made up for in animosity.

Scripture tells us that there's a proper time and place for the display of righteous anger (see Ephesians 4:26), but this was not righteous anger, nor was it the proper time or place. What Job needed was a helping hand, not a slap in the face!

Warren Wiersbe writes:

> How sad it is when people who should share ministry end up creating misery. . . . How tragic that these three friends focused on Job's words instead of the feelings behind those words. A Chinese proverb says, "Though conversing face to face, their hearts have a thousand miles between them." How true that was at the ash heap! After all, information is not the same as communication. Sydney J. Harris reminds us, "Information is giving out; communication is getting through."[1]

Do you feel as though the heart of someone you love is a thousand miles from yours right now? If so, why do you think this is the case? What steps can you take to narrow this distance between you?

We can get information from any source; what we need when we're suffering is the comfort and close communication of someone who truly cares. We want someone to "get through" to us, to speak to us in the depths of our need.

Second, *Zophar accused Job of being ignorant of God:*

> But would that God might speak,
> And open His lips against you,
> And show you the secrets of wisdom!
> For sound wisdom has two sides.
> Know then that God forgets a part of your iniquity.
> Can you discover the depths of God?
> Can you discover the limits of the Almighty?
> They are high as the heavens, what can you do?
> Deeper than Sheol, what can you know?
> Its measure is longer than the earth
> And broader than the sea.
> If He passes by or shuts up,
> Or calls an assembly, who can restrain Him?
> For He knows false men,
> And He sees iniquity without investigating.
> An idiot will become intelligent
> When the foal of a wild donkey is born a man. (Job 11:5–12)

The word *idiot* used in Job 11:12 comes from a Hebrew word meaning "to be hollow or empty." Zophar accused Job of being an "empty-headed idiot." We might use the colloquial term "airhead." Zophar went even further to suggest that there is no more possibility that an idiot like Job could ever become wise than that a donkey could give birth to a man. Can you imagine? Job's lost his home, his children, his servants, his livelihood, and his health. He's in enormous pain and covered with oozing, worm-infested boils. He can't sleep. He can't eat. And now, of all things, he's being called an "empty-headed idiot" by one of his closest friends.

Zophar and his friends acted as though they had a corner on the market when it came to wisdom! They felt fully confident that they knew how God worked—and that Job didn't. Warren Wiersbe comments,

> Zophar wanted Job to grasp the height, depth, breadth, and length of God's divine wisdom (11:8–9). In saying this, Zophar was hinting that he himself already knew the vast dimensions of God's wisdom and could teach Job if he would listen.[2]

What did Zophar wrongly imply about Job in these verses?

How could Zophar have responded more sensitively to Job's needs?

Third, *Zophar accused Job of being stubborn in his refusal to repent.* He instructed Job in the way that he should approach God:

> If you would direct your heart right
> And spread out your hand to Him,
> If iniquity is in your hand, put it far away,
> And do not let wickedness dwell in your tents;
> Then, indeed, you could lift up your face without moral defect,
> And you would be steadfast and not fear.
> For you would forget your trouble,
> As waters that have passed by, you would remember it.
> Your life would be brighter than noonday;
> Darkness would be like the morning.
> Then you would trust, because there is hope;
> And you would look around and rest securely.
> You would lie down and none would disturb you,
> And many would entreat your favor.
> But the eyes of the wicked will fail,
> And there will be no escape for them;
> And their hope is to breathe their last. (Job 11:13–20)

In addition to implying that Job's suffering was a direct result of sin, Zophar over-simplified Job's problems. In what ways did he do this?

Have you ever had anyone downplay or oversimplify a problem you were dealing with? If so, how did this make you feel? How did you respond?

Zophar delivered a lecture in Theology 101—as if Job needed another lecture. And, unfortunately, quite a few Zophars are still on the loose today. If you haven't met one, just wait. He or she will come along, with absolutely no capacity to "connect the dots" or discern your real need. Zophars don't understand how God is working in your life, yet they have a customized message of shame and blame for you . . . and they may even say it's from God. Why do they do this? Because you are not doing what they believe you should be doing. Or you're doing what they believe you should *not* be doing.

How should we respond to such unkind accusations? Let's read on to see how Job was able to model a godly response to his friend's words.

Job's Response to Zophar

In the Disney movie *Bambi,* a young rabbit named Thumper teaches Bambi an important lesson: "If you can't say something nice, don't say anything at all." What great advice! In fact, Job ended up telling his friends essentially the same thing:

> O that you would be completely silent,
> And that [your silence] would become your wisdom! (Job 13:5)

In the book of Proverbs, we find several poignant reminders of the importance of restraining our words. For example:

He who restrains his words has knowledge,
And he who has a cool spirit is a man of understanding.
Even a fool, when he keeps silent, is considered wise;
When he closes his lips, he is considered prudent. (Proverbs 17:27–28)

Zophar should have known that it's better not to speak at all than to heap abuse on someone who has already suffered enough. His silence would have been a welcome relief for Job. But he chose to speak, and instead of taking it on the chin, Job responded to his friend's false accusations.

Job answered each count brought against him by maintaining that he was still upright, blameless, and faultless in his integrity. He knew he was not completely sinless, yet he had been faithful to offer up sacrifices to atone for not only his own sin, but for that of his entire family. So he boldly offered three counterarguments to Zophar's accusations.

First, *Job refuted Zophar's accusation that he had no knowledge of God.* Job affirmed in chapter 12 that he did possess wisdom and understanding, just as his friends did. He had followed God, worshiped Him, and obeyed Him. He admitted that he didn't understand the earthly reason for his suffering, but he held on to his faith.

Second, *Job responded to Zophar's accusation that he was a guilty sinner.* In chapter 13, Job affirmed his integrity and his blameless position before God. In fact, he must have *wished* that he had something to confess, if that would have meant that God would hear his voice and restore him! Yet he still maintained his innocence.

Third, *Job closed his speech by challenging Zophar's suggestion that he could have hope if he simply confessed his sinfulness.* Job admitted that he was close to losing hope, but only because he had no sin to confess. Since he couldn't see the big picture, he begged God to show up and to offer him some perspective on his suffering.

Thomas à Kempis once said, "How rarely we weigh our neighbor in the same balance in which we weigh ourselves."[3] Zophar simply lashed out with his assumptions. In the end, both Job and God reprimanded Zophar, Eliphaz, and Bildad for their lack of compassion.

Warren Wiersbe writes,

"It could be worse!" is certainly no comfort to a man who has lost his family, his wealth, and his health, and is barely hanging on to life. . . . The flippant way in which Job's friends were speaking about his situation shows they lacked understanding. "The deeper the sorrow," says the Jewish *Talmud,* "the less tongue it has."[4]

If you're on the receiving end of poor advice and hurtful accusations, take heart! As Christians, we're called to be gracious and loving, but we're *not* called to be doormats. Jesus modeled kindness and meekness, but He most certainly wasn't afraid to rebuke the Pharisees and chase the money changers out of the temple when necessary.

We aren't obligated to take the advice of every legalistic, joy-stealing person that comes down the pike. We're neither ignorant nor unimportant. We're sons and daughters of the Most High God! No one has the right to mistreat us, shame us, or take advantage of us.

Make it a point to spend time with those who comfort, support, and encourage you in your walk with God. If those around you offer only negativity, unhealthy peer pressure, discouraging and hurtful words, and a lack of sensitivity to your physical, emotional, and spiritual needs, then you may need to get out of your comfort zone and make some new friends!

NUGGETS OF WISDOM

The difficult dialogue between Zophar and Job in chapters 11 through 14 raises three significant questions that each of us needs to answer: a question of depth (Job 11:7–8), a question of discovery (Job 13:9), and a question of destiny (Job 14:14).

First, *are you seeking to know the depths of God?* We often tend to just skim the surface instead of taking risks and plumbing the depths of God's wisdom, knowledge, and grace. Because we feel obligated to "put on a happy face," we often fake spiritual joy instead of being real about our griefs, trials, struggles, and painful disappointments. We tend to make happiness the goal of our Christian lives rather than glorifying God no matter the cost. Author Larry Crabb notes, "We're more attracted to sermons, books, and conferences that reveal the secrets to fulfillment in everything we do than to spiritual direction that leads us through affliction into the presence of the Father."[5]

We can seek to know the depths of God by cultivating intimacy with Him. In fact, He's waiting to hear from us!

> Patiently and graciously [our Lord] waits to reveal insights and dimensions of truth to those who care enough to probe, to examine, to ponder.
>
> Such searching is not merely an intellectual pursuit. God's ways are not discovered through the normal, humanistic methods of research. . . .

As important and intriguing as divine depths might be, they defy discovery by the natural means of our minds. He reserves these things for those whose hearts are completely His . . . for those who take the time to wait before Him. Only in that way can there be intimacy with the Almighty. . . .

Like the great apostle [Paul], let's make this our "determined purpose" [see Philippians 3:10 AMP]. Let's deliberately embrace this aim: to "become more intimately acquainted with Christ."[6]

Read Jesus' words in Matthew 6:33. How can you seek to know God more deeply?

How can you be more real in admitting your disappointments to others?

Second, *will all be well when God examines your life?* Or will it be a disappointing discovery? Scripture says that each of us will stand before the judgment seat of Christ to give an account of the things we have done (see 2 Corinthians 5:10). We'll be held accountable for our actions and our decisions, and only those who have established a relationship with Jesus Christ through faith in Him will enter heaven.

When God examines your life, what positive things will He see? What attitudes and actions would you like to change before you give an account of your life to Him?

Third, *when you die, will you enter God's presence, or will you be separated from Him forever?* As far as we know, only four things are eternal: God, His Word, angels, and people. He made us to live forever. The question is, where? Will we live eternally in heaven with Him, or in hell without Him? In the New Testament, the words *Hades* and *gehenna* refer to *hell,* a term that in common usage designates the place of eternal retribution for those who do not have a relationship with God. Christ Himself referred to the reality of a fiery hell numerous times (see Matthew 5:22, 29–30; 10:28; 18:9; 23:15, 33; Mark 9:43, 45, 47; and Luke 12:5).[7]

Read the passages listed above. What do they tell us about the reality of hell?

What warnings does Jesus give to nonbelievers in these passages?

Clearly, hell is very real, and none of us wants to end up there! Jesus reassures us that those who believe in Him and trust in Him for salvation will have eternal life with Him (John 5:24).

Read Matthew 5:12, 6:9; Acts 1:11; 4:12; and Philippians 3:20. What do these passages tell us about the reality of heaven?

Taking Truth to Heart

If you have placed your trust in Jesus Christ as your personal Lord and Savior, you can rest assured that you will be with God in eternity, not in hell. However, if you have not established a relationship with Him or you are not sure about your salvation, place your trust in Him now. Pray to Him and ask for Him to come into your heart and your life. He comes with His love and His assurance that you are now His child.

If you need guidance in praying to receive Christ, pray a simple "ABC" prayer: *admit* the fact that you're a sinner; *believe* in the Word of God, and recognize that Jesus died for your sins; and *confess* your inability to gain salvation through your own works. Then express your faith in Jesus Christ and your desire for a personal relationship with Him, and ask God to guide you in your new walk with Christ.

If you've prayed to receive Christ today, seek out a pastor or trustworthy Christian individual who can help you grow in your newfound faith and who can answer any questions you may have. In addition, find a church in your community where you can worship God, grow in faith and knowledge, and fellowship with other believers.

If you desire more information on establishing a relationship with Christ or want to talk with someone at Insight for Living about the decision you've made or any other issues, please call our counseling line at (972) 473-5097. We'll be happy to help you plumb the depths of God and find encouragement, wisdom, and tangible support for your journey of faith.

9 *Graceless Words for a Grieving Man*

Selections from Job 15–17

> ## Sorry comforters are you all.
>
> ### —Job 16:2

THE CHORUS OF A POPULAR SPIRITUAL SAYS, "Ev'rybody talkin' 'bout heaven ain't goin' there." In other words, a lot of people *talk* about heaven and *think* they're going there, but some of them are in for a surprise! Jesus says in Matthew 7:21, "Not everyone who says to Me, 'Lord, Lord,' will enter the kingdom of heaven, but he who does the will of My Father who is in heaven will enter."

It's the same with grace, isn't it? We talk about grace all the time, but when it comes to actually offering it to others, we often end up singing a different tune—just like Job's friends. Unfortunately for Job, they knew the tune of "un-grace" by heart!

TREASURES FROM THE TEXT

In chapters 15 through 21 of Job, we find the second cycle of speeches from Job's friends.

> During this second round of speeches, the fire grew hotter as the three friends focus more on proving Job wrong than on giving him help. After all, their own peace of mind was at stake, and they were not about to surrender. If Job was not a sinner being punished by God, then the three friends' understanding of God was all wrong. *But that meant they had no protection against personal suffering themselves!* If obedience is not a guarantee of health and wealth, then what happened to Job might happen to them. God forbid![1]

In chapter 15, Eliphaz sharply rebukes Job, and in chapters 16–17, Job replies. Eliphaz's speech brings to light five characteristics of those who lack grace—pride, a tendency to hurl insults, the use of guilt-inducing tactics, a condemning attitude, and words of sarcasm.

First, *Eliphaz had a haughty manner and a proud heart.* He began his self-righteous speech by suggesting that he knew exactly what Job should *not* do:

> Should a wise man answer with windy knowledge
> And fill himself with the east wind? (Job 15:2)

Eliphaz's tirade consisted of a series of rhetorical questions meant to silence Job's protests of innocence before God. This friend's pride, coupled with his suggestion that Job was "full of hot air" and speaking words that meant nothing, contributed to a speech that was less than comforting for Job. Instead, it discouraged and humiliated him.

Second, *Eliphaz insulted Job.* He called Job's words "useless talk," "not profitable," and "irreverent." He even suggested that Job hindered others' meditation before God:

> Should he argue with useless talk,
> Or with words which are not profitable?
> Indeed, you do away with reverence
> And hinder meditation before God. (Job 15:3–4)

Third, *Eliphaz implied that Job was guilty of sin.* He suggested that Job was simply receiving his just deserts for that sin. Eliphaz also called Job "crafty," insinuating that he was acting in a sneaky, underhanded manner instead of confessing his "hidden sin":

> For your guilt teaches your mouth,
> And you choose the language of the crafty.
> Your own mouth condemns you, and not I;
> And your own lips testify against you. (Job 15:5–6)

Fourth, *Eliphaz condemned Job.* He suggested that Job presumed to "own wisdom" and that Job took a "better-than-thou" attitude toward his friends. In addition, Eliphaz's bitter words revealed that he had been envious all along of Job's close, blessed relationship with the

Lord. Now, he was finally letting Job know what he thought. In fact, he seemed almost pleased to see calamity befall Job! He asked:

> Were you the first man to be born,
> Or were you brought forth before the hills?
> Do you hear the secret counsel of God,
> And limit wisdom to yourself?
> What do you know that we do not know?
> What do you understand that we do not? (Job 15:7–9)

Fifth, *Eliphaz used sarcasm and harsh words to lash out at Job.* Eliphaz saw himself as God's messenger, sent to give Job the advice that he so desperately needed to hear! Unbelievably, Eliphaz actually said that his words were "spoken gently" (Job 15:11):

> Both the gray-haired and the aged are among us,
> Older than your father.
> Are the consolations of God too small for you,
> Even the word spoken gently with you?
> Why does your heart carry you away?
> And why do your eyes flash,
> That you should turn your spirit against God
> And allow such words to go out of your mouth?
> What is man, that he should be pure,
> Or he who is born of a woman, that he should be righteous?
> Behold, He puts no trust in His holy ones,
> And the heavens are not pure in His sight;
> How much less one who is detestable and corrupt,
> Man, who drinks iniquity like water! (Job 15:10–16)

In Job 15:17–35, Eliphaz continued to expound upon the reasons for Job's misery, loss, and anguish. We're stunned by the callousness of Job's so-called friend, yet his style of communication is not that unusual for those who lack grace. Their hearts are filled with pride and a condemning attitude. They use guilt-inducing tactics, hurl insults, and wield words of sarcasm. With friends like that, who needs enemies?

Why is the use of sarcasm evidence of a heart that lacks grace? What effect does it have on those who receive it?

Think over the characteristics of Eliphaz listed above. Which of these might you find yourself portraying if you aren't careful? How is grace the opposite of these characteristics?

In Other Words

One author tells this story about a poignant lesson he learned in grace-giving:

> I remember a mini-paradigm shift I experienced one Sunday morning on a subway in New York. People were sitting quietly—some reading newspapers, some lost in thought, some resting with their eyes closed. It was a calm, peaceful scene.
>
> Then suddenly, a man and his children entered the subway car. The children were so loud and rambunctious that instantly the whole climate changed.
>
> The man sat down next to me and closed his eyes, apparently oblivious to the situation. The children were yelling back and forth, throwing things, even grabbing people's papers. It was very disturbing. And yet, the man sitting next to me did nothing.
>
> It was difficult not to feel irritated. I could not believe that he could be so insensitive as to let his children run wild like that and do nothing about it, tak-

ing no responsibility at all. It was easy to see that everyone else on the subway felt irritated, too. So finally, with what I felt was unusual patience and restraint, I turned to him and said, "Sir, your children are really disturbing a lot of people. I wonder if you couldn't control them a little more?"

The man lifted his gaze as if to come to a consciousness of the situation for the first time and said softly, "Oh, you're right. I guess I should do something about it. We just came from the hospital where their mother died about an hour ago. I don't know what to think, and I guess they don't know how to handle it either."

Can you imagine what I felt at that moment? My paradigm shifted. Suddenly I *saw* things differently, and because I *saw* differently, I *thought* differently, I *felt* differently, I *behaved* differently. My irritation vanished. I didn't have to worry about controlling my attitude or my behavior; my heart was filled with the man's pain. Feelings of sympathy and compassion flowed freely. . . . Everything changed in an instant.[2]

What an important reminder for us to be grace givers! We often don't know the pain and sorrow that others may be experiencing or the hurtful situation that may be causing them to speak or act in a certain way. Let's make it a point to offer a kind word and a helping hand to those around us who may be desperately in need of grace.

Name a time when your perspective on a situation changed once you found out more information. What happened? How did your attitude change once you saw this situation through new eyes?

Job's Reply to Eliphaz

Chapters 16 and 17 contain Job's pointed response to Eliphaz's stinging verbal assault. Job's reply can be divided into four parts.

First, *Job expressed disgust with his so-called friends.* In Job 16:1–5, Job truthfully and pointedly confronted his friends to let them know that they were not achieving their stated purpose of bringing him sympathy, comfort, and encouragement. In verse 2, he bluntly said, "Sorry comforters are you all." Instead of easing Job's pain, his friends' words only increased his sorrow.

Second, *he was distressed by the way God was treating him.* In Job 16:6–17, Job described God as a fierce warrior intent on destroying him. He perceived the Lord as angry, actively seeking to bring suffering and despair on him. Job was distressed by the way he'd been treated, and he struggled to maintain his faith in the face of God's silence and distance.

Third, *he was depressed over his prospects in life.* Job cried:

> My spirit is broken, my days are extinguished,
> The grave is ready for me.
> Surely mockers are with me,
> And my eye gazes on their provocation. (Job 17:1–2)

In other words, "I've reached the breaking point. God's silent, and I can't figure Him out. When I pray, I don't get answers. When I devote myself even more deeply to doing His will for all the right reasons, I continue to lose, and the heavens are brass. God's disappeared." Job had hit bottom and maintained only a shred of hope that he would ever emerge from the depths of his depression and despair.

Fourth, *he was despondent, seeing the grave as nearer than ever.* In Job 17:3–16, Job mourned the fact that life as he once knew it was over. He said:

> But He has made me a byword of the people,
> And I am one at whom men spit. . . .
> My days are past, my plans are torn apart,
> Even the wishes of my heart. (Job 17:6, 11).

Taking the place of Job's former dreams was a feeling of hopelessness:

> Where now is my hope?
> And who regards my hope?

> Will it go down with me to Sheol [the grave]?
> Shall we together go into the dust? (Job 17:15–16)

Job didn't mince words! He expressed his emotions fully and cried out to God for answers. Don't you appreciate the fact that the Bible is full of stories about real people who faced real trials? Life's not a fairy tale full of handsome knights in shining armor charging up on their white steeds to rescue beautiful damsels in distress from their castle-tower prisons. Life's tough, and not everyone lives happily ever after.

Not only that, but as time goes on, life doesn't get easier; it gets harder. Marriage becomes more difficult. Our careers grow more demanding. Child rearing gets more complicated. Our dreams and goals become harder to achieve. Our responsibilities multiply. Our losses mount. We flounder spiritually. Our health gets worse.

That's why Christ died and rose on our behalf—because we can't make it through this life on our own. We need God's grace to redeem us because we're utterly unable to measure up to His standards of righteousness on our own merit. We need the eternal hope that only faith in Christ's sacrificial death and resurrection can give us. And we need peace and hope for today that comes only through a growing, vibrant personal relationship with Jesus.

Taking Truth to Heart

A professor at a Christian college in Missouri once gave his students a penetrating, unforgettable picture of grace. A student from his class wrote this in an e-mail:

In the spring of 2002, I left work early so I could have some uninterrupted study time before my final exam in the Youth Ministry class at Hannibal-LaGrange College in Missouri. When I got to class, everybody was doing their last-minute studying. The teacher came in and said he would review with us before the test. Most of his review came right from the study guide, but there were some things he was reviewing that I had never heard. When questioned about it, he said they were in the book and we were responsible for everything in the book. We couldn't argue with that.

Finally it was time to take the test.

"Leave them face down on the desk until everyone has one, and I'll tell you to start," our professor, Dr. Tom Hufty, instructed.

When we turned them over, to my astonishment every answer on the test was filled in. My name was even written on the exam in red ink. The bottom of the last page said: "This is the end of the exam. All the answers on your test are correct. You will receive an A on the final exam. The reason you passed the test is because the creator of the test took it for you. All the work you did in preparation for this test did not help you get the A. You have just experienced . . . grace."

Dr. Hufty then went around the room and asked each student individually, "What is your grade? Do you deserve the grade you are receiving? How much did all your studying for this exam help you achieve your final grade?"

Then he said, "Some things you learn from lectures, some things you learn from research, but some things you can only learn from experience. You've just experienced grace. One hundred years from now, if you know Jesus Christ as your personal Savior, your name will be written down in a book, and you will have had nothing to do with writing it there. That will be the ultimate grace experience."[3]

You may be thinking, "Why didn't I have a teacher like that when I was taking my final exams?" Most of us probably never had a teacher like that, but we *do* have a heavenly Father like that. Thank goodness for His grace!

Take a few moments now to write down some ways that you have experienced God's mercy and grace.

Now, let's dig into the parable in Matthew 20:1–16, where Jesus dramatically illustrates the power of grace:

For the kingdom of heaven is like a landowner who went out early in the morning to hire laborers for his vineyard. When he had agreed with the laborers for a denarius for the day, he sent them into his vineyard. And he went out about the third hour and saw others standing idle in the market place; and to those he said, "You also go into the vineyard, and whatever is right I will give you." And so they went. Again he went out about the sixth and the ninth hour, and did the same thing. And about the eleventh hour he went out and found others standing around; and he said to them, "Why have you been standing here idle all day long?" They said to him, "Because no one hired us." He said to them, "You go into the vineyard too."

When evening came, the owner of the vineyard said to his foreman, "Call the laborers and pay them their wages, beginning with the last group to the first." When those hired about the eleventh hour came, each one received a denarius. When those hired first came, they thought that they would receive more; but each of them also received a denarius. When they received it, they grumbled at the landowner, saying, "These last men have worked only one hour, and you have made them equal to us who have borne the burden and the scorching heat of the day. But he answered and said to one of them, "Friend, I am doing you no wrong; did you not agree with me for a denarius? Take what is yours and go, but I wish to give to this last man the same as to you. Is it not lawful for me to do what I wish with what is my own? Or is your eye envious because I am generous?" So the last shall be first, and the first last.

With whom in this parable do you most closely identify, and why?

Do you feel that the landowner was fair or unfair to those who had worked all day? Why?

What does this parable teach us about God's grace?

Do we ever really want "fair" from God, or do we want mercy and grace instead? What would "fair" from God look like for us?

NUGGETS OF WISDOM

Those who feel distressed, depressed, and despondent need two things. First, *they need grace for the moment.* They need to know that God's there, that He's listening, that He loves them, and that in His Word He promises them an abundant life. They may need you to provide them with a safe place to share their feelings. And the Lord may call you to make sacrifices to help a loved one through a crisis or a period of grief or suffering.

Second, *they need hope for the future.* Job teaches us much about the importance of faith and the value of hope in helping us deal with difficult trials. In his book *Disappointment with God,* Phillip Yancey tells this story in which he compares a friend's predicament with Job's:

> Once a friend of mine went swimming in a large lake at dusk. As he was paddling at a leisurely pace about a hundred yards offshore, a freak evening fog rolled in across the water. Suddenly he could see nothing: no horizon, no landmarks, no objects or lights on shore. . . .
>
> For thirty minutes he splashed around in panic. He would start off in one direction, lose confidence, and turn ninety degrees to the right. Or left—it made no difference which way he turned. He could feel his heart racing uncontrollably. He would stop and float, trying to conserve energy, and force himself to breathe slower. Then he would blindly strike out again. At last he heard a faint voice calling from shore. He pointed his body toward the sounds and followed them to safety.
>
> Something like that sensation of utter lostness must have settled in on Job as he sat in the rubble and tried to comprehend what had happened. He too had lost all landmarks, all points of orientation. Where should he turn? God, the One who could guide him through the fog, stayed silent. . . .
>
> God ultimately won The Wager, of course. Though Job lashed out with a stream

of bitter complaints, and though he despaired of life and longed for death, still he defiantly refused to give up on God: "Though he slay me, yet will I hope in him." Job believed when there was no reason to believe. He believed in the midst of the fog.[4]

When have you felt like you were "in the fog," with nowhere to turn?

Did you eventually feel God guiding you out of the fog, or did a friend or family member offer you a lifeline? If so, how?

Job struggled with feelings of despair, but he was able to maintain a shred of hope despite it all. What do you think enabled Job to maintain his hope in the fog of his suffering?

Do you know anyone who seems to be struggling through a fog right now? If so, what can you do to offer this person encouragement, direction, and comfort?

Jesus says, "You are the light of the world. A city set on a hill cannot be hidden. . . . Let your light shine before men in such a way that they may see your good works, and glorify your Father who is in heaven" (Matthew 5:14, 16). You serve as the light of the world, called to offer grace to those in a world of "un-grace." Make it a point to be a grace giver!

10 Reassuring Hope for the Assaulted and Abused

Selections from Job 18–19

> As for me, I know that my Redeemer lives,
> And at the last He will take His stand on the earth.
>
> —Job 19:25

AN OLD PROVERB SAYS, "A real friend is someone who walks in when the rest of the world walks out."[1] By this time, the rest of the world had already walked out on Job. He desperately needed a real friend—someone who understood, someone who sympathized, someone who was on his side.

Mother Teresa once said, "Kind words are short and easy to speak, but their echoes are truly endless."[2] Unfortunately, the echoes of *unkind* words are endless, also. All of us can remember painful words and actions of others that occurred years ago. Some of these hurts are so fresh in our minds that they seem like they happened just yesterday! As we examine Bildad's angry words and read Job's frustrated reply, we'll see just how important it is to speak kind, supportive words to those we love.

TREASURES FROM THE TEXT

In chapter 18, Bildad launches into his second hurtful speech. In verses 1 through 4, he takes off the kid gloves and reaches an all-time low in his hurtful accusations toward Job.

> Then Bildad the Shuhite responded,
> "How long will you hunt for words?
> Show understanding and then we can talk.
> Why are we regarded as beasts,

> As stupid in your eyes?
> O you who tear yourself in your anger—
> For your sake is the earth to be abandoned,
> Or the rock to be moved from its place?" (Job 18:1–4)

Not an encouraging start! Next, in verses 5–21, Bildad reminds Job of the many terrors that death brings, painting four vivid portraits of the horrifying circumstances that await the wicked.

Four Portraits

Portrait One: *Bildad compares Job to a light that has gone out.*

> Indeed, the light of the wicked goes out,
> And the flame of his fire gives no light.
> The light in his tent is darkened,
> And his lamp goes out above him. (Job 18:5–6)

Notice that Bildad openly calls Job "wicked." Bildad, in his faulty thinking, believes that a lack of blessing always indicates wickedness, because God always punishes the wicked in the present. Conversely, he also believes that blessing always indicates uprightness, because God always blesses the righteous in the here and now. Bildad's message to Job is: "If you repent, God will bless you. If you don't repent, He'll keep judging you." But Bildad's theology doesn't leave any room for the mystery of God's will and God's ways, which may not be apparent in the moment.

This "friend" suggests that Job's suffering means that he's out of God's will. But such cause-and-effect logic fails in Job's case—and in many others' as well. Christ's suffering on the cross was the Father's perfect will (Acts 2:23). So was Paul's thorn in the flesh, which God used for specific purposes in the apostle's life.

Read 2 Corinthians 12:7–10. What were God's purposes in giving Paul this thorn in the flesh?

What can Paul's experience tell you about Job's suffering?

What can Paul's experience tell you about suffering you have endured or currently endure?

Portrait Two: *Bildad compares Job to a trapped traveler.*

> His vigorous stride is shortened,
> And his own scheme brings him down.
> For he is thrown into the net by his own feet, . . .
> And a trap snaps shut on him.
> A noose for him is hidden in the ground,
> And a trap for him on the path. (Job 18:7–10)

Bildad suggests that by refusing to confess some hidden sin, Job has set a trap for himself. He implies that Job has a "scheme" that he's not admitting or confessing.

Why do you think Job's friends kept urging him to confess sin? How were they over-simplifying his situation?

Portrait Three: *Bildad compares Job to a pursued criminal.*

> All around terrors frighten him,
> And harry him at every step.
> His strength is famished,
> And calamity is ready at his side.
> His skin is devoured by disease,
> The firstborn of death devours his limbs.
> He is torn from the security of his tent,
> And they march him before the king of terrors.
> There dwells in his tent nothing of his;
> Brimstone is scattered on his habitation. (Job 18:11–15)

"The king of terrors"—what a name for death! According to Bildad, death stands at Job's door, ready to seize him and reduce him to nothing. Bildad even dares to suggest that "brimstone," associated with hell and direct punishment from God (see Genesis 19:24) will fall upon Job, just as fire had fallen upon Job's sons and daughters (Job 1:16).

Portrait Four: *Bildad compares Job to an uprooted tree.*

> His roots are dried below,
> And his branch is cut off above.
> Memory of him perishes from the earth,
> And he has no name abroad.
> He is driven from light into darkness,
> And chased from the inhabited world.
> He has no offspring or posterity among his people,

Nor any survivor where he sojourned.
Those in the west are appalled at his fate,
And those in the east are seized with horror.
Surely such are the dwellings of the wicked,
And this is the place of him who does not know God. (Job 18:16–21)

Bildad calls Job a tree with dried-up roots and cut-off branches—a sharp contrast with the scriptural picture of a wise and godly man who remains rooted like a mighty tree (see Psalm 1:3). Bildad reminds Job that he has lost all his children; he also intimates that the entire world is horrified by Job's fate. He ends by again calling Job "wicked" and "him who does not know God" (Job 18:21).

Bildad's Mistakes

In his speech, Bildad makes two major mistakes:

1. *Bildad speaks to the wrong man.* It's true that the horrors of death will be great for a person who does not know God. The Bible says that these people will be separated from the Lord forever and be cast into eternal torment. But these accusations should not have been made against a faithful man. Since Job had known God and had walked closely with Him, he knew that he would not have to face the terrors of death and hell (see Job 19:25). He had hope for a much better life waiting for him in heaven. He even longed for death so that he could meet Almighty God and finally be free from his torment.

2. *Bildad speaks with a wrong motive.* He brings abuse, insults, and advice instead of a humble willingness to commiserate with Job in his anguish. Bildad's faulty theology has been challenged as he has seen Job suffering, and his fear must have motivated his harsh words. Proverbs 12:18 tells us, "There is one who speaks rashly like the thrusts of a sword, but the tongue of the wise brings healing." Bildad could have brought his friend healing with kind words of consolation. Instead, his verbal jabs pierced Job's heart like a dagger.

What have you learned from Job's friends about what to say and what not to say when a loved one is hurting?

NUGGETS OF WISDOM

Job's reply, divided into four main stanzas, appears in Job 19. In the first stanza, Job addresses Bildad's insults. In the second, he offers illustrations to describe the depths of his pain. In the third, he depicts his isolation and sorrow. In the fourth, he offers some insight into his unique situation.

Job Addresses Bildad's Insults

> Then Job responded,
> "How long will you torment me
> And crush me with words?
> These ten times you have insulted me;
> You are not ashamed to wrong me.
> Even if I have truly erred,
> My error lodges with me.
> If indeed you vaunt yourselves against me
> And prove my disgrace to me,
> Know then that God has wronged me
> And has closed His net around me." (Job 19:1–6)

Job makes it known that his friend's words have caused him even greater distress and torment. Bildad and the others should have been embarrassed to offer such hurtful advice to a friend who was in such desperate need.

What emotions emerge from Job's reply? What does his response tell you about how he feels?

Job Counters Bildad's Argument with Illustrations

His friend had described four frightening "death scenarios." Job answers with seven vivid pictures of the trials of his life.

> [God] has closed His net around me.
> Behold, I cry, "Violence!" but I get no answer;
> I shout for help, but there is no justice.
> He has walled up my way so that I cannot pass,
> And He has put darkness on my paths.
> He has stripped my honor from me
> And removed the crown from my head.
> He breaks me down on every side, and I am gone;
> And He has uprooted my hope like a tree.
> He has also kindled His anger against me
> And considered me as His enemy.
> His troops come together,
> And build up their way against me
> And camp around my tent. (Job 19:6–12)

The first illustration appears at the end of 19:6—Job feels like a trapped animal with a net closed around him. He announces that God has wronged him by laying a trap of suffering for him.

Second, Job claims that he has been wronged like an innocent person taken to court. He pleads for justice and cries out for a mediator or advocate to defend him before God (19:7).

Third, Job feels like a fenced-in traveler (19:8). God has walled up his passageway so he cannot get through. In addition, he says the Lord has removed the light from his path so he can't see.

Fourth, Job's suffering has left him feeling like a dethroned king (Job 19:9). Job had once enjoyed God's blessing, peace, wealth, and prosperity. Now, he's been stripped of his honor and blessing. His "royal robes" have been reduced to rags, and his "crown" has been replaced with the ashes of suffering.

Fifth, his life is like a building that's been destroyed (19:10). Job feels that God has broken him down like the walls of a condemned building, reducing his entire life to rubble.

Sixth, Job's hope has been uprooted like a tree (19:10; also see 18:16). Job feels that his hope, instead of blossoming like the beautiful, firmly rooted tree referred to earlier, is more like a discarded tree that's no longer fruitful.

Seventh, Job compares himself to a city besieged by a fierce enemy (19:11–12). He feels that the Lord's anger is kindled against him and that God considers him an enemy. He describes God as a warrior, gathering his troops and charging toward his object of conquest.

What do these illustrations tell you about Job's perception of God? Was this perception accurate? Why or why not?

What picture or illustration would you use to describe how God is working in your life right now?

Job mourns his isolation from God, friends, and family members that had once been so near and dear to him:

> He has removed my brothers far from me,
> And my acquaintances are completely estranged from me.

My relatives have failed,
And my intimate friends have forgotten me.
Those who live in my house and my maids consider me a stranger. . . .
My breath is offensive to my wife,
And I am loathsome to my own brothers.
Even young children despise me;. . . .
All my associates abhor me,
And those I love have turned against me.
My bone clings to my skin and my flesh,
And I have escaped only by the skin of my teeth.
Pity me, pity me, O you my friends,
For the hand of God has struck me.
Why do you persecute me as God does,
And are not satisfied with my flesh? (Job 19:13–15, 17–22)

In this passage, how does Job depict his isolation?

Have you ever felt a deep sense of isolation? If so, when? What did you learn about God during this time?

One author writes,

Job closed this part of his defense by appealing to his friends for pity (vv. 21–22; 6:14). God was against him, his family and friends had deserted him, and all he had left were his three intimate friends who were now pursuing him like wild beasts after their prey. Couldn't they stop and try to help him? Why must they have such hard hearts?[3]

Why do you think Job's friends had such hard hearts?

Are there people in your life whose suffering has elicited hard-heartedness on your part? What about their situation or circumstances has caused you to recoil rather than reach out?

In the latter part of chapter 19, Job offers Bildad some insight into his situation:

> Oh that my words were written!
> Oh that they were inscribed in a book!
> That with an iron stylus and lead
> They were engraved in the rock forever!
> As for me, I know that my Redeemer lives,
> And at the last He will take His stand on the earth.
> Even after my skin is destroyed,
> Yet from my flesh I shall see God;
> Whom I myself shall behold,
> And whom my eyes will see and not another. (Job 19:23–27)

Taking Truth to Heart

Musicians, writers, and artists have focused much attention on this magnificent passage containing Job's passionate faith statement and his cry for justice. Christian recording artist Nicole C. Mullen sings a powerful song called "Redeemer" based on verse 25. Also, in Handel's classic oratorio *Messiah,* the soprano sings a breathtaking aria based on Job 19:25–26 and 1 Corinthians 15:20:

I know that my Redeemer liveth,
and that he shall stand at the latter day upon the
earth: and though worms destroy this body,
yet in my flesh shall I see God.
For now is Christ risen from the dead,
the first fruits of them that sleep.[4]

Warren Wiersbe writes this about the Job passage:

In 19:25–27, Job expressed confidence that, even if he died, he would still have a Redeemer who one day would exercise judgment on the earth. Furthermore, Job affirmed that he himself expected to live again and see his Redeemer! "And after my skin has been destroyed, yet in my flesh I will see God" (v. 26, NIV). It was an affirmation of faith in the resurrection of the human body.

The Hebrew word translated "Redeemer" in verse 25 refers to the kinsman redeemer, the near relative who could avenge his brother's blood (Deut. 19:6-12), reclaim and restore his brother's property (Lev. 25:23–24, 39–55), and set his brother free from slavery (25:25). The kinsman redeemer could also go to court on behalf of a wronged relative (Prov. 23:10–11). In the Book of Ruth, Boaz is the kinsman redeemer who was willing and able to rescue Ruth and give her a new life in a new land.[5]

The picture of the kinsman-redeemer foreshadows the coming of Christ, our Redeemer. Though Job does not know Christ, he recognizes God as his Redeemer. He feels wronged, yet he knows that God is still sovereign. Despite his suffering, he believes that his only hope is to cling to his faith in the Almighty. Job trusts that, whether in this life or the next, he will stand rightly before God.

Verses 28 and 29 contain a fierce concluding warning from Job to his friends:

> If you say, "How shall we persecute him?"
> And, "What pretext for a case against him can we find?"
> Then be afraid of the sword for yourselves,
> For wrath brings the punishment of the sword,
> So that you may know there is judgment. (Job 19:28–29)

Job rebukes them for their lack of mercy and announces that they will be judged for their wrongful accusations against him.

Refer to Romans 8:1, 33–34. Is there any place for condemnation of God's children? Is there a place for Spirit-led, loving admonition in the Christian life? Why or why not?

How has the Lord shown mercy to you through the words and actions of those around you?

Take a few minutes to pray now, thanking the Lord for His presence, His comfort, His grace, and His mercy to you. Let the memories of His faithfulness to you serve as a reminder to offer grace and hope to others.

Responding Wisely When Falsely Accused

Selections from Job 20–21

> ## Can anyone teach God knowledge,
> ## In that He judges those on high?
>
> —Job 21:22

IT'S SURPRISING how often false accusations appear in Scripture. Potiphar's wife wrongly accused Joseph of rape, and he wound up in jail. Saul falsely accused David of trying to dethrone him. Nehemiah was accused of rebuilding the walls around Jerusalem in order to make himself king. Some Christians accused Paul of undergoing a false conversion as a means of trapping and betraying them. And Jesus Himself faced endless false accusations from the chief priests, scribes, and religious leaders.

Job also faced his share of hurtful falsehoods as his friend Zophar hurled insults at him like darts toward a bull's-eye. Job endured the verbal onslaught, but he didn't allow Zophar to take advantage of him. He listened to Zophar's accusations, then shot a pointed retort right back at his accuser.

TREASURES FROM THE TEXT

Zophar Again Accuses Job

In Job 20, Zophar made three postulations about the fate of the wicked. First, Zophar asserted that *the wicked do not live long.* In Job 20:2–11, Zophar described the evil that befalls those who do not place their faith in God (by inference, Job):

> Then Zophar the Naamathite answered,
> "Therefore my disquieting thoughts make me respond,

111

Even because of my inward agitation.
I listened to the reproof which insults me,
And the spirit of my understanding makes me answer.
Do you know this from of old,
From the establishment of man on earth,
That the triumphing of the wicked is short,
And the joy of the godless momentary?
Though his loftiness reaches the heavens,
And his head touches the clouds,
He perishes forever like his refuse;
Those who have seen him will say, 'Where is he?'
He flies away like a dream, and they cannot find him;
Even like a vision of the night he is chased away. . . .
His bones are full of his youthful vigor,
But it lies down with him in the dust." (Job 20:2–8, 11)

Zophar declared that the wicked's triumph has always been brief. He suggested that God intervenes quickly to punish evil. Yet, throughout Scripture, this is rarely the case; the Lord often waits to send judgment upon evildoers. He waited 120 years before sending the Flood (Genesis 6:3). He waited over 400 years to judge the Amorites (Genesis 15:12–16). In His grace, He frequently allows ample time for repentance before destroying the wicked.

In fact, Christians throughout the ages have lamented that God has not stepped in quickly enough to punish evildoers. But that's God's grace! His mercy and His lovingkindness toward us cause Him to delay His wrath upon sin. The apostle Peter wrote: "The Lord is not slow about His promise, as some count slowness, but is patient toward you, not wishing for any to perish but for all to come to repentance" (2 Peter 3:9).

Paul reminds us of our Father's kindness and patience in the book of Romans: "Or do you think lightly of the riches of His kindness and tolerance and patience, not knowing that the kindness of God leads you to repentance?" (Romans 2:4).

God never promised the faithful an easy, trouble-free life. In fact, the most godly people in Scripture had to endure periods of deep and difficult suffering. Zophar's assumptions were based on human reasoning, not God's ways of dealing with people.

In what ways has God exercised His kind patience toward you?

Is there someone in your life toward whom God wants you to be patient and extend mercy?

Second, Zophar warned that *the pleasures of the wicked are temporal, for the wicked (that is, Job) face an early death:*

> Though evil is sweet in his mouth
> And he hides it under his tongue,
> Though he desires it and will not let it go,
> But holds it in his mouth,
> Yet his food in his stomach is changed
> To the venom of cobras within him.
> He swallows riches,
> But will vomit them up;
> God will expel them from his belly.
> He sucks the poison of cobras;
> The viper's tongue slays him. . . .
> He returns what he has attained
> And cannot swallow it;
> As to the riches of his trading,
> He cannot even enjoy them.
> For he has oppressed and forsaken the poor;
> He has seized a house which he has not built. (Job 20:12–16, 18–19)

Zophar utilized a metaphor comparing the evildoer's enjoyment of sin to the consumption of food. According to him, the wicked man enjoys sin the way one might enjoy a delicious feast. But eventually that sin poisons his system. Wrongdoing carries with it both temporary enjoyment and punishment; if you want the one, you must also accept the other.

Third, Zophar implied that *suffering is always the result of God's judgment on the wicked.* In the next verses, Zophar painted a terrifying picture of the judgment and punishment that the wicked will receive:

> Complete darkness is held in reserve for [the wicked man's] treasures,
> And unfanned fire will devour him;
> It will consume the survivor in his tent.
> The heavens will reveal his iniquity,
> And the earth will rise up against him.
> The increase of his house will depart;
> His possessions will flow away in the day of His anger.
> This is the wicked man's portion from God,
> Even the heritage decreed to him by God. (Job 20:26–29)

Not even the rich man's wealth and prosperity can keep death from his door. Zophar said God will chase him down and pierce him with a bronze-tipped arrow (Job 20:24). He will be captured and dragged into court, where heaven and earth will testify against him and find him guilty as charged (Job 20:27).

Zophar accused Job of offering a wicked man's heritage as opposed to a godly heritage. How can you offer a godly heritage to those within your sphere of influence?

Job Replies

Job took on Zophar's accusations, first by saying, *"Listen to me!"*

> Then Job answered,
> > "Listen carefully to my speech,
> > And let this be your way of consolation." (Job 21:1–2)

Job said, in effect, "I've listened to you long enough. Now you listen to me for a change!" To his credit, he had allowed his friend to speak his mind, even though Zophar's accusing words had made Job's emotional wounds hurt even more. But now, it was Job's turn to speak, and he wasn't about to mince words!

Next, Job told Zophar, *"Bear with me."*

> Bear with me that I may speak;
> Then after I have spoken, you may mock.
> As for me, is my complaint to man?
> And why should I not be impatient? (Job 21:3–4)

Job no longer expected sympathy, but only the opportunity to be heard. He pointed out that his complaint was not against men but against God. He felt impatient and wronged because none of his friends had helped him, and God had not answered him. And the longer God waited to speak, the worse Job's situation seemed to become.

Job then exclaimed, *"Look at me!"*

> Look at me, and be astonished,
> And put your hand over your mouth.
> Even when I remember, I am disturbed,
> And horror takes hold of my flesh. (Job 21:5–6)

Job commanded his friend to stop lecturing into space and look him in the eye. No doubt, Job's appearance was so horrible that Zophar could barely stand to look at him. But Job wanted him to speak to his face instead of standing and judging at a distance or murmuring about him behind his back.

Ever notice that false accusers don't like to make their accusations to our faces? Instead, they tend to sneak around in the shadows. They talk about us behind our backs. They seek out people who are weak, gullible, and willing to listen to half-truths, and then they infect those people with their "verbal germs." Jesus said that those with nothing to hide seek the light, but those who deal in wickedness prefer to stay in the darkness (John 3:19–21). Job finally said to Zophar, "You've talked about me long enough. It's time for me to speak up and clear up these false accusations you've been spreading!"

Job Refutes Zophar's Accusations

Job refuted each of the three statements Zophar made in chapter 20 regarding the fate of the wicked.

First, Job stated that *often, the wicked do live long lives.*

> Why do the wicked still live,
> Continue on, also become very powerful?
> Their descendants are established with them in their sight,
> And their offspring before their eyes,
> Their houses are safe from fear,
> And the rod of God is not on them.
> His ox mates without fail;
> His cow calves and does not abort.
> They send forth their little ones like the flock,
> And their children skip about.
> They sing to the timbrel and harp
> And rejoice at the sound of the flute.
> They spend their days in prosperity. . . .
> They say to God, "Depart from us!
> We do not even desire the knowledge of Your ways." (Job 21:7–14)

Job reminded Zophar that sometimes the wicked *do* prosper. They don't all die off at age twenty but live long lives and even enjoy good health and success. People don't necessarily suffer on earth just because they aren't godly. In all likelihood, most of the world's elite do not have a personal relationship with God. While Christians are promised an abundant life, we're not promised a *perfect* life. In fact, believers may face more trials and suffering than others do because Satan opposes the pursuit of our goal. But our hope lies in our eternal life with the Father—not in temporal health, wealth, and prosperity on earth.

Read Hebrews 11:24–26. As the son of Pharaoh's daughter, what kind of life could Moses have chosen? What did he value and choose instead?

How did it benefit Moses to follow God's ways? In the same way, despite his suffering, what blessings had Job received in his life as a result of his decision to follow God?

Next, Job stated that *the wicked do not always suffer calamity.*

> How often is the lamp of the wicked put out,
> Or does their calamity fall on them?
> Does God apportion destruction in His anger?
> Are they as straw before the wind,
> And like chaff which the storm carries away?
> You say, "God stores away a man's iniquity for his sons."
> Let God repay him so that he may know it. (Job 21:17–19)

Rewards for the Christian and punishment for the non-Christian aren't black-and-white—at least in this life. After death, we know that those who love God and have a personal relationship with Him will enter heaven, while those who do not will enter hell. But on earth, things are less clear-cut. A lost person may have a beautiful family, a successful career, plenty of money, a yacht, and multiple homes. He or she may drink, smoke, sleep around, have a wild lifestyle, and live to be one hundred. In contrast, many Christians around the world don't even have bread to eat, water to drink, or a roof over their heads, and they may leave earth much sooner.

The question is, how do we measure true fulfillment? Do we measure it according to our levels of worldly happiness, which may soar one day and sink the next? Or are we assessing true, God-given joy and peace? Are we comparing our material possessions to those of others, or do we count as riches the abundant hope of our eternal life with Christ? Jesus taught us:

> Do not store up for yourselves treasures on earth, where moth and rust destroy, and where thieves break in and steal. But store up for yourselves treasures in heaven, where neither moth nor rust destroys, and where thieves do not break in or steal; for where your treasure is, there your heart will be also. (Matthew 6:19–21)

Where is your treasure (and your heart) right now? In what ways do you compare your life and possessions to those of others?

How can you remind yourself of God's blessings and appreciate the riches you have in Christ?

Last, Job reminded Zophar that often, *the death of the wicked is no different from the death of other men.*

> Can anyone teach God knowledge,
> In that He judges those on high?
> One dies in his full strength,
> Being wholly at ease and satisfied;
> His sides are filled out with fat,
> And the marrow of his bones is moist,

While another dies with a bitter soul,
Never even tasting anything good. (Job 21:22–25)

Job picked up on the "eating" metaphor that Zophar introduced earlier. But he maintained that some people live long lives getting fat on succulent food, while others live difficult lives begging for crumbs. His point? Death comes for us all.

Job continued his sharp response to Zophar's misguided counsel:

For the wicked is reserved for the day of calamity;
They will be led forth at the day of fury.
Who will confront him with his actions,
And who will repay him for what he has done?
While he is carried to the grave,
Men will keep watch over his tomb.
The clods of the valley will gently cover him;
Moreover, all men will follow after him,
While countless ones go before him.
How then will you vainly comfort me,
For your answers remain full of falsehood? (Job 21:30–34)

Job told Zophar: "Your theology is too simplistic. It doesn't mesh with reality. I'm not in the category with the wicked!" Job saw that, wicked or righteous, some die comfortable and wealthy, while some die bitter and in anguish. And only God understands the reasons why.

We've seen enough to know that those who love God don't always live long, outwardly blessed lives, and the wicked don't always live short, miserable lives. It just doesn't seem fair, does it? But we know that we can trust the heart of God to bring good from every situation. Every trial that we endure strengthens and matures us, conforming us to the image of Christ (James 1:2–4). Without suffering, how could we relate to our Savior, who endured the greatest of all suffering on our behalf?

NUGGETS OF WISDOM

Those of us who have been falsely accused know that the human tongue can be the most treacherous of enemies. Hurtful words can cause more emotional damage and heartache than any other source of trouble. What we say cuts far deeper than any knife or sword. James wrote:

> The tongue is a small part of the body, and yet it boasts of great things.
> See how great a forest is set aflame by such a small fire! And the tongue is a fire, the very world of iniquity; the tongue is set among our members as that which defiles the entire body, and sets on fire the course of our life, and is set on fire by hell. . . . No one can tame the tongue; it is a restless evil and full of deadly poison. With it we bless our Lord and Father, and with it we curse men, who have been made in the likeness of God; from the same mouth come both blessing and cursing. My brethren, these things ought not to be this way. (James 3:5–6, 8–10)

The Bible describes the tongue as a destructive fire blazing a path through others' lives, causing deep, lingering hurt and lasting scars. It's no surprise that we find this mandate in the Ten Commandments: "You shall not bear false witness against your neighbor" (Exodus 20:16).

When Solomon wrote Proverbs, he included a list of seven things that God hates. Among them is "a false witness who utters lies" (Proverbs 6:19). The Lord despises falsehood, yet liars are still on the loose, even in Christian circles. If you've borne the brunt of someone's lies or been falsely accused, you know what it's like to feel real, undeserved pain. And you've discovered how difficult it can be to defend yourself. You may have tried to set the record straight, but the venom of poisonous tongues had already taken its toll.

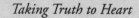

Taking Truth to Heart

We all need wisdom and courage to know how to stand up to such painful false accusations. From Job 20–21, we can glean four guidelines for having a godly response when we're falsely accused.

Stay calm. Listen to what is being said, considering the nature of the critic. Take everything you hear with a grain of salt and respond carefully. If someone makes you angry or falsely accuses you, take time to cool off before approaching that person. And don't repeat anything to others that is hurtful or untrue. If you're not sure, err on the side of caution and stay silent.

Speak truth. If someone accuses you personally, weigh the pros and cons of responding to that person versus keeping silent and letting the situation blow over. Be sure you have proof of the person's hurtful words or actions before confronting him or her. Take time to prayerfully consider what your godly response should be. Then, if you believe God is calling you to do so, confront the person in a gracious, loving, and calm manner. Remind him or her that your relationship is important to you, and that you don't want any hard feelings or misunderstandings to come between the two of you. Also, express your confidence by stating that you know he or she would not want to spread false information, and you want to set the record straight.

In addition, if you hear someone speaking lies or spreading gossip about others, you may be called to confront that person in love to keep him or her accountable for his or her words and actions. Calmly and lovingly getting to the root of an issue can keep the weeds of gossip from growing and choking out the fruit in your life and in the lives of your loved ones.

Lean hard on the Lord. In the past, perhaps someone accused you of something and you weren't able to confront him or her. As a result, you may have carried an undeserved damaged reputation or the knowledge that others had wrong ideas about you. When you face hurtful accusations such as these, trust your defense to the Lord. Pray for wisdom and strength to deal with the problem and stay rooted in Scripture. Seek Christian counsel if necessary. This can provide you with a lifeline if you feel you're drowning in a sea of false accusations.

Get tough. Refuse to let the accusations discourage and derail you. An old Revolutionary War motto says, "Trust in God, but keep your powder dry!" In other words, trust God, but stay sharp and ready for battle against Satan and his devices. Don't be afraid to address problems or false accusations when they arise. Rumors are like ticking time bombs; the sooner you defuse them, the better off you'll be. Use the spiritual discernment God gives you through the Holy Spirit. And use your common sense, too! As much as possible, avoid people and situations that you know could lead to gossip or rumors.

What situations in your life seem to breed gossip or unwarranted talk about others?

What can you do to defuse these situations?

Often situations involving false accusations seem insurmountable. Yet God knows our hearts and our deepest hurts. His Son, Jesus, felt the sting of insults and bitter betrayal, too. God understands human pain better than we realize, and He is our Judge and our Defender. Even if everyone in the world believes a lie, our Father knows the truth. And He loves us completely!

12 How to Handle Criticism with Class
Selections from Job 22–24

But He knows the way I take;

When He has tried me, I shall come forth as gold.

—Job 23:10

PULITZER PRIZE-WINNING WRITER Ernest Hemingway defined *courage* as "grace under pressure."[1] Many of the world's greatest leaders have demonstrated grace under pressure as they faced opposition, insults, and criticism from those around them. One such leader was the brilliant and colorful Sir Winston Churchill, who not only handled criticism with class, he invited it. Biographer Steven Hayward verifies this:

> Although Churchill's supreme self-confidence always led him to believe he could persuade his colleagues about the course of action he favored, he always sought criticism and advice from his colleagues and subordinates. One of his aides at the Treasury in the 1920s said of Churchill that "He always took criticism very, very meekly. One could say exactly what one liked in the way of criticism. . . . He wanted the full critical value from subordinates." . . .
>
> Despite Churchill's tendency to dominate meetings with his volubility, he always encouraged a complete discussion of issues, and never penalized or fired anyone from openly or vigorously disagreeing with him. "Opportunity was always given for full discussion," one of his wartime aides wrote. Lord Bridges wrote after the war, "I cannot recollect a single Minister, serving officer or civil servant who was removed from office because he stood up to Churchill and told Churchill that he thought his policy or proposals were wrong." Moreover, Churchill never overruled the service chiefs of staff, even when he strenuously disagreed with their decisions.[2]

Churchill knew how to handle criticism with class. He exhibited grace under pressure!

Those three words could be written across every page of the book of Job. Though loss bankrupted him, the death of his ten children grieved him, disease ravaged him, and his alleged friends criticized and berated him, Job courageously endured.

TREASURES FROM THE TEXT

Eliphaz Steps into the Ring

In the third cycle of debate, Eliphaz stepped into the ring once more, swinging both fists. His criticism started to sound like the same song, third verse as he proceeded to make more false accusations against Job.

First, *Eliphaz falsely accused Job of sin:*

> Is not your wickedness great,
> And your iniquities without end?
> For you have taken pledges of your brothers without cause,
> And stripped men naked.
> To the weary you have given no water to drink,
> And from the hungry you have withheld bread. . . .
> You have sent widows away empty,
> And the strength of the orphans has been crushed.
> Therefore snares surround you,
> And sudden dread terrifies you,
> Or darkness, so that you cannot see,
> And an abundance of water covers you. (Job 22:5–7, 9–11)

Instead of trying to calm things down, Eliphaz assumed the position of the prosecuting attorney and turned the debate into a trial. Like any effective attorney, he had his brief prepared and his case well in hand. His false accusations, however, described someone the exact opposite of Job.

Eliphaz reasoned that courts don't try people for being righteous or for obeying the law. Rather, they try people for breaking the law. Therefore, he falsely deduced that since Job had received such terrible punishment, he must be guilty of sin.

Next, *Eliphaz accused Job of hiding his sins:*

> Is not God in the height of heaven?
> Look also at the distant stars, how high they are!
> You say, "What does God know?
> Can He judge through the thick darkness?
> Clouds are a hiding place for Him, so that He cannot see;
> And He walks on the vault of heaven."
> Will you keep to the ancient path
> Which wicked men have trod,
> Who were snatched away before their time,
> Whose foundations were washed away by a river?
> They said to God, "Depart from us!"
> And "What can the Almighty do to them?" (Job 22:12–17)

Others who heard the comments of Eliphaz must have thought, "These certainly are some pointed accusations! We never noticed Job committing all these sins." That's because Job didn't commit them! But Eliphaz asserted that Job was guilty and that he had simply hidden his sinful deeds from public view.

In Job 22:12–14, Eliphaz reminded Job that he couldn't hide anything from God. He warned Job in verses 15 through 18 that his so-called sins would be discovered. In essence, he called Job a hypocrite.

What exactly is a hypocrite? The dictionary defines the term as "a person who puts on a false appearance of virtue or religion."[3] Warren Wiersbe writes,

> [Eliphaz suggested that] Job was a hypocrite, a statement that was made—or hinted at—more than once since the discussion began. "The hypocrite's hope shall perish," said Bildad (8:13). "For the congregation of hypocrites shall be desolate," said Eliphaz (15:34). And Zophar said, "The joy of the hypocrite [is] but for a moment" (20:5).
>
> A hypocrite is not a person who fails to reach his desired spiritual goals, because all of us fail in one way or another. A hypocrite is a person who doesn't even try to reach any goals, but *he makes people think that he has.* His profession and his practice never meet.[4]

What situations or expectations make you feel pressured to put on a false appearance? Why?

Last, *Eliphaz exhorted Job to repent of his sins:*

> Yield now and be at peace with Him;
> Thereby good will come to you.
> Please receive instruction from His mouth
> And establish His words in your heart.
> If you return to the Almighty, you will be restored;
> If you remove unrighteousness far from your tent,
> And place your gold in the dust . . .
> Then the Almighty will be your gold
> And choice silver to you. (Job 22:21–25)

Here, Eliphaz delivered a great evangelistic message—he just delivered it to the wrong person! Put yourself in Job's position. You're a believer, yet others accuse you of being wicked and headed straight for hell. You're blameless and upright, yet you're faced with brutal taunts and false allegations. You have a choice. Will you demonstrate godly grace under pressure? Or will you strike back with a verbal weapon?

Job chose the former. He handled himself with class, and he neither lashed back nor overreacted as he answered his critic.

Job's Reply

Job's reply, found in chapters 23 and 24, consists of three candid, calm, and vulnerable responses. Incredibly, Job did not interrupt Eliphaz. He did not protest or answer back until Eliphaz was finished. Then, Job spoke to and about the Lord instead of directly addressing

Eliphaz or his accusations. Job knew that it was not Eliphaz who would justify him, but the Lord. He longed for God to bring about justice in his case.

Job began by saying, *"I am unable to locate the presence of God."*

> Oh that I knew where I might find Him,
> That I might come to His seat!
> I would present my case before Him
> And fill my mouth with arguments.
> I would learn the words which He would answer,
> And perceive what He would say to me.
> Would He contend with me by the greatness of His power?
> No, surely He would pay attention to me.
> There the upright would reason with Him;
> And I would be delivered forever from my Judge.
> Behold, I go forward but He is not there,
> And backward, but I cannot perceive Him;
> When He acts on the left, I cannot behold Him;
> He turns on the right, I cannot see Him.
> But He knows the way I take;
> When He has tried me, I shall come forth as gold.
> My foot has held fast to His path;
> I have kept His way and not turned aside.
> I have not departed from the command of His lips;
> I have treasured the words of His mouth more than my necessary food. (Job 23:3–12)

Job was desperate for God to show Himself. But even though God hadn't allowed Job's circumstances to improve, Job trusted the Lord to listen to his concerns (Job 23:4) and to offer him a response (23:5). He believed that God would take seriously his pleas for justice (23:6), hear his arguments, and clear his record (23:7). Yet Job admitted that he couldn't literally see, or behold, God (23:8–9).

Do you ever feel as if you can't find God or that He seems far away? Read John 14:20; 1 Corinthians 6:17; and 1 Peter 5:7. What promises do you find?

When you *feel* that God's far away, what does He want you to trust about Him, His presence, and His care for you?

Next, Job said, *"I am unable to understand the plan of God."*

> But He is unique and who can turn Him?
> And what His soul desires, that He does.
> For He performs what is appointed for me,
> And many such decrees are with Him.
> Therefore, I would be dismayed at His presence;
> When I consider, I am terrified of Him. (Job 23:13–15)

If the doctrine of God's sovereignty is supposed to be such a source of strength for His people, then why was Job so frightened by it? Perhaps because his suffering had made him realize that he had no control over his own life; God did. He didn't know about the cosmic wager that had set him up for such tremendous trials, and he feared what might happen next. He trembled before his Creator, yet he knew that his only hope of salvation and restoration remained in God's hands. Job trusted God, though he could not understand His ways.

Job demonstrated incredible trust in God even though he lived before seeing the promise of Christ's birth, death, and resurrection fulfilled. What does the cross of Christ tell us about God's heart toward us at all times (see Romans 8:31–32)?

Last, Job admitted, *"I am unable to justify God's permissions."* In chapter 24, Job offered examples of the blatant injustice that God allows in the world. He described unfairness that occurs in the country:

> Why are times [of judgment] not stored up by the Almighty,
> And why do those who know Him not see His days?
> Some remove the landmarks;
> They seize and devour flocks.
> They drive away the donkeys of the orphans;
> They take the widow's ox for a pledge.
> They push the needy aside from the road;
> The poor of the land are made to hide themselves altogether. . . .
> Others snatch the orphan from the breast,
> And against the poor they take a pledge.
> They cause the poor to go about naked without clothing,
> And they take away the sheaves from the hungry. (Job 24:1–4, 9–10)

And in the city:

> From the city men groan,
> And the souls of the wounded cry out;
> Yet God does not pay attention to folly.
> Others have been with those who rebel against the light;
> They do not want to know its ways
> Nor abide in its paths.
> The murderer arises at dawn;

He kills the poor and the needy,
And at night he is as a thief.
The eye of the adulterer waits for the twilight,
Saying, "No eye will see me."
And he disguises his face. (Job 24:12–15)

How did Job feel about the fact that crimes and exploitation abounded, but God seemed to do nothing about it? What was Job's point in describing these injustices?

Finally, Job explains *the curses that fall upon the wicked:*

[The wicked] are insignificant on the surface of the water;
Their portion is cursed on the earth.
They do not turn toward the vineyards. . . .
They are exalted a little while, then they are gone;
Moreover, they are brought low and like everything gathered up;
Even like the heads of grain they are cut off.
Now if it is not so, who can prove me a liar,
And make my speech worthless? (Job 24:18, 24–25)

Eventually the wicked will meet their fate and their evil activities will come back to haunt them. Job detested those who disobeyed God's laws and yet seemed to escape judgment.

Which specific curses did Job say would befall the wicked? What would these people's outcome be?

Despite his own painful trials and losses, Job focused his attention in these verses on the suffering of others in his community. What does this tell you about his character?

Job was concerned not only with his own vindication and restoration, but also with that of others around him. He recognized that when people suffer physically, they also suffer spiritually and emotionally. They, like Job, long for comfort and encouragement. They want answers. They need to know that people care and that God is present.

Jesus recognized this essential need in His earthly ministry. He addressed personal and spiritual issues by feeding people, teaching them, healing them, and ministering to their physical needs. Rather than spending all His time dealing with theoretical issues and philosophical problems, *Jesus Christ loved people.* He wasn't afraid to reach out and touch them, and in so doing, He radically and tangibly changed their lives forever.

In Other Words

All of us struggle at times to demonstrate grace when we're under pressure. Author David Roper describes the essence of such grace and the benefits of learning obedience through pressure-inducing trials:

Our Lord was nailed to the cross; you can count on being nailed to the wall. It's helpful to see each ordeal that way—as being crucified with Christ. . . .

God gives us over to such bruisings because they are part of the process to make us what he intends us to be. The hurting makes us sweeter, more mellow. We lose the fear of losing out; we learn to let go of what we want. We're not so easily provoked to wrath by harm or reproof. We learn to absorb abuse without retaliation, to accept reproof without defensiveness, to return a soft answer to wrath. It makes us calm and strong.[5]

NUGGETS OF WISDOM

Zophar has shown us how *not* to respond to those who hurt. So how can we respond in a way that brings restoration and healing instead? From our study of these three chapters of Job, we can draw three lessons about how to comfort others who face unfair criticism and unexplained suffering.

First, *resist the temptation to explain everything.* When you ask a question, wouldn't you prefer to hear someone honestly admit, "I don't know!" rather than make up a half-hearted answer? One man has said that an education is moving from unawareness to awareness of our ignorance. The older we get, the more we learn; but the more we learn, the more we realize our limitations.

Sometimes, our friends or family members experience hurts that we can't explain. But we *can* be there. This story illustrates the importance of being available:

> Tragedy struck one family when the mother died abruptly and early, leaving behind a loving husband and young daughter. The father and the daughter were suddenly left with only the memory of this wonderful wife and mother. Their grief and sorrow went deep. The night following the funeral, as the father tucked his daughter in bed, his heart went out to her, seeing that she was fighting back the tears. He decided that he would move a cot into her room so he could comfort her. He pulled it up close beside his daughter's bed, and they soon fell asleep.
>
> In the middle of the night, the father awoke to the sound of his daughter crying. He spoke comforting words to her, and through her tears she said, "Daddy, it's so hard. I just miss her so much." Fighting back his own tears, he reached over and took her hand. She said, "Oh, that's so much better." And she put her hand over his shoulder and leaned against his chest. Wanting to comfort her, he said, "You know, sweetheart, we have the Lord to lean on." She said, "I know that, Daddy . . . but tonight I just need someone with skin on."

We don't always know the reasons behind others' suffering, but we can be "God with skin on" to comfort them when they hurt.

Second, *focus on future benefits, not the present pain.* Despite his pain, Job looked toward the future. He felt confident that even though he was being tried in the white-hot fire, he would come forth as gold (Job 23:10). He maintained his innocence even when falsely accused, knowing that in this life or the next, he would eventually receive a reward for enduring his suffering.

What benefits come from suffering and difficult times?

Third, *embrace the sovereignty of God.* We tend to think that we can't embrace someone or something we don't understand. But we do it all the time! We love our spouses and kids, but we don't completely understand them. We have loving relationships with our parents and friends, in spite of the fact that we don't know everything there is to know about them. We accept mystery and allow time for growth in our relationships with others, so reason demands that we must expect these aspects in our relationship with our Father as well.

How have you glimpsed God's sovereignty in your life? How have you felt the depths of His love and compassion?

Do you ever think of God as jealous for your love, attention, and devotion? The Scriptures say that He is (see Exodus 34:14; Deuteronomy 5:9). The kind of jealousy ascribed to God is a holy, positive jealousy that longs for your *full* devotion.

How does this fact affect your life?

How do you show your gratitude for the sacrificial love God has offered you through Jesus Christ?

Like Job, we see only the earthly aspects of our situation, while God understands the heavenly aspects. Only He sees the big picture. Just as we can't fully know God until we reach heaven, we can't fully know why certain situations occur on earth. Some things surpass the scope of our limited human knowledge. But we can trust God's heart, knowing that His love for us surpasses understanding like a doting father's care for his child.

The next time you face harsh or unfair criticism, remember that you can always find assurance, acceptance, love, and peace in the presence of the Almighty.

13 *The Futility of Unscrewing the Inscrutable*

Job 25–26

> How faint a word we hear of Him!
> But His mighty thunder, who can understand?
>
> —Job 26:14

THE STUDY OF JOB is also the study of God. After all, God is the one who strikes the deal with Satan. It's He who points out Job as a God-fearing, blameless man and allows the enemy to unleash his arrows. Then the Almighty steps into the shadows and hides for 35 chapters! He no longer speaks. He doesn't give visions. He doesn't provide relief. He doesn't offer comfort. Not only is He absent, He's silent. And that's tough for Job (and us) to understand. All the way through the story, it is God who captures our attention and makes us wonder. Better stated, He *confuses* us.

Those of us who grew up attending Sunday school and church may have been taught that God is good, merciful, gracious, kind, and just. And He is! He "sympathize[s] with our weaknesses" (Hebrews 4:15), "knows what you need before you ask Him" (Matthew 6:8), and "satisfies your years with good things" (Psalm 103:5). Remember the little prayer you may have recited as children at mealtime? "God is great. God is good. Let us thank Him for this food. Amen." And that was that.

But then we dig into the book of Job, and we're confused. The simplistic "health and wealth" theology that many of us have been taught just doesn't mesh with the details of Job's life. As we delve more deeply into the book, we realize that we must have misunderstood either the person of God or the person of Job. Most likely, our concept of God needs to be reshaped.

TREASURES FROM THE TEXT

Bildad's Speech

Job 25 records Bildad's shortest speech to date. In fact, Bildad offered the most concise soliloquy in the entire book as he expounded on the inferiority of man and the superiority of God. But what his speech lacked in length, it certainly made up for in jabs and accusations. Specifically, Bildad's words focus our attention on two aspects of God's nature.

1. *Bildad referred to God's power and greatness.* He attempted to strike fear into Job's heart by painting a verbal picture of Yahweh's awesome capabilities.

> Then Bildad the Shuhite answered,
> "Dominion and awe belong to Him
> Who establishes peace in His heights.
> Is there any number to His troops?
> And upon whom does His light not rise?" (Job 25:1–3)

Bildad portrayed God as a fierce warrior who demonstrates His power and majesty to His subjects in order to keep the peace. He described the Lord as high and unknowable. Bildad's speech brings to mind the words of the Lord spoken through the prophet Isaiah, "'For My thoughts are not your thoughts, nor are your ways My ways,' declares the LORD" (Isaiah 55:8). This passage reminds us of the lofty inscrutability of God's ways.

Digging Deeper

What does it mean to be *inscrutable?* The dictionary defines the term as "not readily investigated, interpreted, or understood."[1] The apostle Paul wrote, "Oh, the depth of the riches both of the wisdom and knowledge of God! How unsearchable are His judgments and unfathomable His ways!" (Romans 11:33). Take a moment to ponder two words in Paul's second sentence. *Unsearchable. Unfathomable.* Consider their full weight in your mind.

In the first century, when Paul penned his letter, he informed his readers that God is *unfathomable* and *unsearchable.* That doesn't mean He stops being good, or loving, or merciful. He's all of that and so much more. But His mind and His plan often remain incomprehensible to us—wonderfully incomprehensible. For just as God's plan through the Messiah was greater than the nation of Israel ever expected, so what He is accomplishing in our lives is greater than we'll ever expect.

The longer we think on this, the more we realize that there is a lot about God we were never taught. In the midst of our study of Job, we're forced to dig much deeper into His character and discover new aspects. And this is a never-ending process! The more we get to know Him, the more He amazes us and inspires awe within us. He is *inscrutable.*

This story helps us grapple with what inscrutable means:

One of the first times I remember that word [*inscrutable*] making a dent in my brain occurred when I was graduating from seminary in the spring of 1963. The president of Dallas Seminary was the late Dr. John F. Walvoord, a man I always admired for his clear-thinking, theological mind. He told our graduating class that he would hope all of us would continue to remember that our God is inscrutable. He then quoted Romans 11:33. Looking around the campus chapel audience, he added with a wry smile, "There will be times you will try to unscrew the inscrutable. You cannot do so!" As usual, Dr. Walvoord was right. But we so want to. Everything within us longs to explain everything about God and interpret all His ways and to come to a full understanding of the workings of God.[2]

After all, God created us as intelligent beings, and He instructs us to know Him. Longing to do that, we continue to pursue a deeper understanding of His divine Being, but the deeper we dig, the more unfathomable He becomes. That shouldn't surprise us, but we're dissatisfied by not knowing. We prefer things to be "fathomable," or, if you will, "scrutable." We want to analyze and explain situations so that we can see the big picture and understand the whole story. But that's impossible when it comes to our sovereign, magnificent God.

As Christians, we rightly emphasize knowing God, yet there's so much that we will never know until we meet the Lord face-to-face in His heavenly kingdom. We don't understand everything about our Father, and we mislead ourselves and others if we imply that we do. One author notes, "Too often, those who say the most about God know the least about God."[3]

Author Warren Wiersbe writes,

The fourteenth-century British spiritual writer Richard Rolle said, "He truly knows God perfectly that finds Him incomprehensible and unable to be known." The more we learn about God, the more we discover how much more there is to know! Beware of people who claim to know all about God, for their claim is proof they know neither God nor themselves.[4]

In what ways *can* you know God? How can you deepen that knowledge?

What aspects and attributes of God are difficult for you to know or understand?

2. *Bildad emphasized God's justice and man's sinfulness.* He asked:

> How then can a man be just with God?
> Or how can he be clean who is born of woman?
> If even the moon has no brightness
> And the stars are not pure in His sight,
> How much less man, that maggot,
> And the son of man, that worm! (Job 25:4–6)

A maggot? A worm? Bildad certainly used some harsh and derogatory terms to describe Job. He focused his put-downs not just on mankind in general, but on Job in particular.

We can make several observations here. This is Bildad's third and last presentation. It is the shortest chapter in the entire book, containing only six verses. And, finally, since Bildad ran out of arguments, he didn't attempt to prove Job wrong. He simply suggested that it's futile to argue with God since He's incomprehensible and His ways are inscrutable.

This was Bildad's perfect chance to remedy the wrongs he and his friends had done to Job. He could have spoken kind words to counteract the painful ones. He could have offered a touch of comfort and encouragement. He could have ministered to his friend's physical, spiritual, and emotional needs. Instead, he chose to deliver a series of sharp barbs that sank deep into Job's heart. It's no wonder that Job offered some stabbing words of his own in return.

Job's Reply

Job had listened to Bildad long enough. All along, Bildad had presumed to be Job's teacher; now, Job would teach him a thing or two! He held Bildad accountable for his discouraging words and actions.

> Then Job responded,
> "What a help you are to the weak!
> How you have saved the arm without strength!
> What counsel you have given to one without wisdom!
> What helpful insight you have abundantly provided!
> To whom have you uttered words?
> And whose spirit was expressed through you?" (Job 26:1–4)

Job had restrained himself to this point, but now he let loose. Pain often has this effect on us. Someone once wrote, "Pain plants the flag of reality in the fortress of a rebel heart." Although we wouldn't consider Job a rebel, pain certainly got his attention and caused him to be more outspoken than usual. When we're hurting, we don't censor our words as much as we normally do. We're honest. We say what needs to be said. Even people who have been stubborn and rebellious are forced to face the facts when their pain intensifies.

One author writes this regarding Job's response:

> Job assumes two roles. The author presents him as a truly righteous man whose commitment to God is total, yet who can still struggle with God to the point of rage

over the mystery of God's ways. Job does not know what the reader knows—that God honors him by testing, thus expressing his total confidence in Job. But Job must remain ignorant of this for it to be genuine. For the intended message of the book, the raging Job is just as important as the patient Job. In his suffering Job served God supremely, not as a stoic, but as a feeling man who had to come to terms with the mystery of the divine.[5]

Job wrestled with pain, rage, and a lack of understanding of God and His ways. Instead of hiding his emotions, Job vented them as he struggled with the enormity of God and his own role in the grand drama of creation. He went on to describe God's majesty and dominion over all He had created.

> The departed spirits tremble
> Under the waters and their inhabitants.
> Naked is Sheol before Him,
> And Abaddon has no covering.
> He stretches out the north over empty space
> And hangs the earth on nothing.
> He wraps up the waters in His clouds,
> And the cloud does not burst under them.
> He obscures the face of the full moon
> And spreads His cloud over it.
> He has inscribed a circle on the surface of the waters
> At the boundary of light and darkness.
> The pillars of heaven tremble
> And are amazed at His rebuke.
> He quieted the sea with His power,
> And by His understanding He shattered Rahab.
> By His breath the heavens are cleared;
> His hand has pierced the fleeing serpent.
> Behold, these are the fringes of His ways;
> And how faint a word we hear of Him!
> But His mighty thunder, who can understand? (Job 26:5–14)

List the images that Job draws from nature to detail God's dominion. What is the main point Job makes with these images?

How do Job's references to creation change our perspective on our lives?

NUGGETS OF WISDOM

Let's examine another example from nature to remind us just how powerful our God is.

To grasp the scene, imagine a perfectly smooth glass pavement on which the finest speck can be seen. Then shrink our sun from 865,000 miles in diameter to only two feet . . . and place the ball on the pavement to represent the sun.

Step off 82 paces (about two feet per pace), and to represent proportionately the first planet, Mercury, put down a tiny mustard seed.

Take 60 steps more, and for Venus put down an ordinary BB.

Mark 78 more steps . . . put down a green pea representing earth.

Step off 108 paces from there, and for Mars put down a pinhead.

Sprinkle around some fine dust for the asteroids, then take 788 steps more. For Jupiter, place an orange on the glass at that spot.

After 934 more steps, put down a golf ball for Saturn. . . .

. . . Mark 2,086 steps more, and for Uranus . . . a marble.

Another 2,322 steps from there you arrive at Neptune. Let a cherry represent Neptune.

This will take two and a half miles, and we haven't even discussed Pluto! If we swing completely around, we have a smooth glass surface five miles in diameter, yet just a tiny fraction of the heavens. . . . Guess how far we'd have to go on the same scale before we could put down another two-foot ball to represent the nearest star. . . .

We'd have to go 6,720 miles. . . . Miles, not feet. . . .

Phenomenal isn't the word for it.[6]

God's creation awes us with its grandeur and brilliance. How can we possibly fathom a God who could create something so vast? Perhaps the question should not be, "Do we really *know* God?" but "Do we really *believe* in Him?" Do we believe what His Word says? Do we recognize His goodness and His love for us? Do we trust Him when circumstances remind us that we're not in control of our own lives? Do we remain faithful to Him even when trials and tests come? Are we grateful to Him for sending His only Son to die for us? Do we live like it?

In Other Words

In his book titled *The Knowledge of the Holy,* A. W. Tozer comments,

Left to ourselves we tend immediately to reduce God to manageable terms. We want to get Him where we can use Him, or at least know where He is when we need Him. We want a God we can in some measure control. We need the feeling of security that comes from knowing what God is like, and what He is like is of course a composite of all the religious pictures we have seen, all the best people we have known or heard about, and all the sublime ideas we have entertained.

If all this sounds strange to modern ears, it is only because we have for a full half century taken God for granted. The glory of God has not been revealed to this generation of men. The God of contemporary Christianity is only slightly superior to the gods of Greece and Rome, if indeed He is not actually inferior to them in that He is weak and helpless while they at least had power.[7]

What are some of the differences between God Almighty and false gods, including the Greek and Roman gods of mythology?

In your life, how have you tried to "reduce God to manageable terms"?

We can't completely know or understand God, and we can't control Him. What do these facts mean for your life?

What do they mean when applied to a current trial for you?

What steps can you take to more intimately know your heavenly Father?

If nothing else, the study of Job reveals that we do not fully understand God's ways. We cannot explain the inexplicable. We cannot fathom the unfathomable. So let's not try to unscrew the inscrutable!

If only the men who saw themselves as Job's friends had acknowledged the limits of human understanding. It would have been so much more comforting to Job to hear his friends say, "We're here. We don't understand why this is happening any more than you do;

only God knows. But we're here to help you and support you through it. God is doing something phenomenal, and it is so far beyond us that we cannot understand it."

God's plan stretches our faith while conforming us to the image of His Son. For some people, His plan may include a long battle with cancer or another terminal illness. For some, like Job, His plan seems to be engaging us in a wrestling match with pain and grief. For others, life may be a struggle with heartbreak, pride, blindness, paralysis, or another hardship.

Often, God's plan is to say no to our requests for healing or a reprieve from our pain. But some of us simply can't accept that. In fact, some go so far as to say, "If you believe that, you lack real faith in God." Truth is, if you believe that, you believe in the God of the Bible!

Scripture describes problems in the lives of many godly people, and often these men and women did not suddenly get well, did not quickly get over their problems, and did not easily overcome failures, sins, accidents, and illnesses. God's Word paints realistic portraits of its heroes—warts and all. They hurt. They fell. They failed. They suffered. But they also learned in the process. By His grace, most of them began to grow, mature in their faith, learn obedience, and succeed in carrying out God's plan for their lives instead of hiding in the shadows, nursing their wounds. And God calls us to do the same.

How can we start to understand the mysteries of God's character and His plan? One way is to get out into the beauty of nature. Let God's creation remind you of His creative power, His imagination, His energy, and His tremendous love for the people and things He has made. Take a prayer walk, using your time to thank Him for the beauty of His creation and the greatness of His power.

In addition, you can grow in your faith and knowledge of Him as you pray, worship, read His Word, journal, fellowship with other believers, and serve in the areas of your spiritual giftedness.

God's foremost command to us is to love Him with all our might. Not just to serve Him, but to love Him for who He is and what He has done for us. When we experience heartaches and setbacks, He's there to comfort us like a loving father comforts his beloved son or daughter. And He deserves our undivided attention and praise. He may be mysterious, but He's mighty, and there's no questioning the vast depths of His love for us.

14 *A Recommitment to Things That Matter*

Selections from Job 27–28

> Till I die I will not put away my integrity from me.
> I hold fast my righteousness and will not let it go.
>
> —Job 27:5–6

SUFFERING HELPS US STRAIGHTEN OUT OUR PRIORITIES. And often, the deeper our pain, the clearer our vision becomes regarding what's truly important in life.

Pastor and author John Piper writes: "Sometimes massive suffering comes so close to home that for a brief season the fog of our foolish security clears, and we can see the sheer precipice of eternity one step away."[1]

Job certainly saw the "precipice of eternity" when his avalanche of horror began, taking the lives of his children, his servants, and his livestock. His circumstances got even worse when his good health suddenly vanished. He lost his livelihood, too, but he didn't mourn the loss of his business the way he grieved over his ten children. The lives of his loved ones mattered much more to him than his possessions.

It's the same today. When disaster strikes, we realize how much we value our relationships with our loved ones. It's rare to hear a successful professional person, suddenly stricken with a life-threatening illness, saying, "I wish I'd spent more time at the office." But that person *is* likely to say, "I wish I'd spent more time at home with my family."

If Job could speak today, he would verify our need to refocus our priorities, urging us to pause and reassess the state of our lives. His children were killed in a freak tornado and his business went belly-up as a result of a cataclysmic series of events. His health went south, his skin erupted with oozing boils, and his fever rose to dangerous levels, yet we never hear Job lament the loss of his fortune or his business. But he did mourn the loss of his family, and he cried out to God for answers in the midst of his grief.

Job's example demonstrates that when it comes to our priorities, suffering is not our enemy; it's our *friend*. Not until we embrace it as such will we reap its benefits. When suffering knocks us flat on our backs, we're forced to look up! We assume a vertical focus instead of a horizontal one. When we're hurting, we allow ourselves to slow down and see our lives from God's point of view. We notice those people and things around us that we've been neglecting. Instead of trying to pull ourselves up by our own bootstraps, we humbly recognize our dependence upon our Father and set our minds on the things of God.

TREASURES FROM THE TEXT

Job Affirms His Righteousness

Chapters 27 and 28 of the book of Job provide an interlude between Job's rebuke of Bildad (chapter 26) and his nostalgic musings on his glorious past (chapter 29). Here Job reaffirmed his righteousness before the Lord and men:

> Then Job continued his discourse and said,
> "As God lives, who has taken away my right,
> And the Almighty, who has embittered my soul,
> For as long as life is in me,
> And the breath of God is in my nostrils,
> My lips certainly will not speak unjustly,
> Nor will my tongue mutter deceit.
> Far be it from me that I should declare you [Bildad] right;
> Till I die I will not put away my integrity from me.
> I hold fast my righteousness and will not let it go.
> My heart does not reproach any of my days." (Job 27:1–6)

Have you noticed that Job always attributed his suffering to the hand of God and not to Satan? Yet, incredibly, he refused to speak unjust or deceitful words against His Creator. He held firmly to his belief that God had a greater purpose behind the scenes. He stood fast in affirming his own integrity, and even went so far as to give a strong oath to support his words: "As God lives" (Job 27:2).

Warren Wiersbe observes, "Among Eastern people in that day, taking an oath was a serious matter. It was like inviting God to kill you if what you said was not true. Job was so sure of himself that he was willing to take that chance.[2]

In verse 2, Job repeated his accusation that God had not treated him fairly. He had asked God to declare the charges against him, yet the Lord had remained silent. Job had begged for an umpire or arbitrator to argue his case before the Almighty but to no avail. So Job continued to hold fast to his principles and defend his integrity, no matter what his friends said or did.

Job Curses His Enemies

In the next several verses, Job uttered a curse against his enemies:

> May my enemy be as the wicked
> And my opponent as the unjust.
> For what is the hope of the godless when he is cut off,
> When God requires his life?
> Will God hear his cry
> When distress comes upon him?
> Will he take delight in the Almighty?
> Will he call on God at all times?
> I will instruct you in the power of God;
> What is with the Almighty I will not conceal.
> Behold, all of you have seen it;
> Why then do you act foolishly? (Job 27:7–12)

In the culture of Job's day, those who suffered typically did more than affirm their innocence; they also called down the wrath of God on their accusers. The "imprecatory Psalms," in which the psalmist sought God's judgment on his enemies, are examples of this type of cursing. To *imprecate* means "to invoke evil on: curse."[3] Sadly, because of their hard hearts and uncaring words, Job's so-called friends had become his spiritual enemies, and he spoke out against them in this passage.

Job taught these men a lesson about the power of God, describing God's righteous judgment of the wicked.

This is the portion of a wicked man from God,

And the inheritance which tyrants receive from the Almighty.

Though his sons are many, they are destined for the sword;

And his descendants will not be satisfied with bread.

His survivors will be buried because of the plague,

And their widows will not be able to weep.

Though he piles up silver like dust

And prepares garments as plentiful as the clay,

He may prepare it, but the just will wear it

And the innocent will divide the silver.

He has built his house like the spider's web,

Or as a hut which the watchman has made.

He lies down rich, but never again;

He opens his eyes, and it is no longer.

Terrors overtake him like a flood;

A tempest steals him away in the night. . . .

Men will clap their hands at him

And will hiss him from his place. (Job 27:13–20, 23)

Windows to the Ancient World

In verse 15, Job noted that the wicked will die, and their widows will not mourn for them. In ancient Near Eastern culture, failure to mourn a person's death would have been the ultimate insult to that person and his or her family. Normally, long and dramatic periods of grief, wailing, and mourning followed the death of a loved one.

Job also reminded his accusers that the children of the wicked will perish by the sword or die from the ravages of the plague. Any who manage to survive these two hazards will spend the rest of their lives begging for food. In addition, the wicked will lie down rich and wake up poor. Their silver and their luxurious, expensive clothing will turn to dust. Their houses will be destroyed, and even their death will be marked by terror rather than peace.

Recognize anything familiar in Job's speech? That's right! He used his friends' own words against them. In this description, he used many of the images that Eliphaz, Bildad, and Zophar had used in their previous judgment speeches against him. Job did this deliberately to remind them that they needed to watch themselves or the punishments they ascribed to others would be applied to them instead. Today we might say, "What goes around comes around!"

The Bible contains numerous examples of people who faced the punishments they had prepared for others. We call this "poetic justice." Author Warren Wiersbe notes:

> Scripture records several instances where the judgment planned by an enemy was brought home to that enemy by the Lord. Pharaoh ordered the newborn Jewish boys to be drowned, and his own army was drowned in the Red Sea (Ex. 1:15–22; 14:23–31). Haman built a gallows on which to hang Mordecai; but Haman and his sons were hanged there instead (Esther 7:10; 9:25). Daniel's enemies tried to have him destroyed, but they and their families ended up in the lions' den in the place of Daniel (Dan. 6:24).[4]

The book of Proverbs also describes this paradox: "The righteous is delivered from trouble, but the wicked takes his place" (11:8).

Job Searches for Wisdom

Following his warning of judgment against his three accusers, Job shifted gears into a discussion of man's search for God's wisdom. It's as if he were saying to his friends, "You need more wisdom from God to discern who is really in danger here." And he recognized his own need for God's wisdom as well.

In chapter 28, Job used rich imagery to explain how difficult it is for man to discern the wisdom of God. He painted vivid images of miners boring deep into the earth, searching for pockets of hidden treasure:

> Surely there is a mine for silver
> And a place where they refine gold.

Iron is taken from the dust,
And copper is smelted from rock.
Man puts an end to darkness,
And to the farthest limit he searches out
The rock in gloom and deep shadow.
He sinks a shaft far from habitation,
Forgotten by the foot. . . .
Its rocks are the source of sapphires,
And its dust contains gold. . . .
He puts his hand on the flint;
He overturns the mountains at the base.
He hews out channels through the rocks,
And his eye sees anything precious.
He dams up the streams from flowing,
And what is hidden he brings out to the light. (Job 28:1–4, 6, 9–11)

List the images that Job used here to illustrate our search for wisdom. What patterns do you see?

How is our search for wisdom like mining treasure?

Job's life offers us a simple yet useful way to describe wisdom: the ability to see life as God sees it. Wisdom means we can interpret events correctly and grasp what they really mean. Wisdom provides us the ability to respond in a positive way to life's challenges. It helps us keep the correct perspective and maintain the right attitude. But finding it is key.

Job continued to expound on the difficulty of the search for wisdom:

But where can wisdom be found?
And where is the place of understanding?
Man does not know its value,
Nor is it found in the land of the living.
The deep says, "It is not in me";
And the sea says, "It is not with me."
Pure gold cannot be given in exchange for it,
Nor can silver be weighed as its price. . . .
Coral and crystal are not to be mentioned;
And the acquisition of wisdom is above that of pearls. . . .
Where then does wisdom come from?
And where is the place of understanding?
Thus it is hidden from the eyes of all living
And concealed from the birds of the sky.
Abaddon and Death say,
"With our ears we have heard a report of it." (Job 28:12–15, 18, 20–22)

Job concluded that God is the origin of wisdom. True wisdom can only come from our Father. It cannot be mined from the earth. It cannot be bought with a price. And it cannot be found through human effort. God Almighty is the only One who understands the nature of wisdom, and He imparts it as a gift to His children.

God understands its way,
And He knows its place.
For He looks to the ends of the earth
And sees everything under the heavens.
When He imparted weight to the wind
And meted out the waters by measure,
When He set a limit for the rain
And a course for the thunderbolt,
Then He saw it and declared it;
He established it and also searched it out.

And to man He said, "Behold, the fear of the Lord, that is wisdom;
And to depart from evil is understanding." (28:23–28)

Job recognized that in the midst of his suffering, God was sovereign. If He had created the world and placed the planets spinning in their orbits, surely He could manage the circumstances of Job's life. Job's role was to trust God's wisdom as perfect, holy, and blameless. The fact that we can't grasp that wisdom only serves to illustrate how much greater God's power and plan are than our own.

NUGGETS OF WISDOM

Job's words in chapters 27 and 28 lead us to make five conclusions about committing to the things that matter most in life. First, *thinking God's thoughts is our highest goal.* A.W. Tozer wrote, "What comes into our minds when we think about God is the most important thing about us."[5]

How do you picture God? If you had to illustrate Him, what would He look like?

What does your illustration idea indicate about your view of God?

What other qualities or attributes come into your mind when you think about God?

There's no better way to know God and think His thoughts than to memorize Scripture. The Bible is God's Word, and His Word is made up of His thoughts. When you determine to bank on His promises or pray for a friend or family member using His words, you can sense the power of biblical truth. God has provided you with the sword of the Spirit, and it's your best weapon against the evil schemes of Satan.

Next, *walking in integrity is the only way to live.* Job's wife and friends suggested that Job take the easy road and admit to doing something he hadn't done. "Oh, Job, just make it easy on yourself. Confess your sin, curse God and die," they told him. But Job refused to skate along on the pond of half-truths. He wouldn't plead guilty to a crime that he hadn't committed. He said in Job 27:4, "My lips certainly will not speak unjustly, nor will my tongue mutter deceit."

Third, *realizing that wrong will not ultimately triumph brings us a sense of justice.* In Job 27:18, Job compared the house of the wicked man to a spider's web. Flimsy and temporary, the habitat of the wicked will be easily destroyed.

Proverbs says:

> Do not weary yourself to gain wealth,
> Cease from your consideration of it.
> When you set your eyes on it, it is gone.
> For wealth certainly makes itself wings
> Like an eagle that flies toward the heavens. (23:4–5)

Ever seen the bumper sticker that says, "He who dies with the most toys wins"? Wrong! He who dies with the most toys only leaves them behind for someone else to enjoy. But godly people recognize that material goods only offer temporary relief and pleasure. God keeps score, and only those who have a true relationship with Him will receive rewards in eternity.

Next, *seeking wisdom through human effort is a waste of time.* We often use the terms *knowledge* and *wisdom* interchangeably. However, they're vastly different! No matter how knowledgeable we may be, we cannot have true biblical wisdom unless we have a relationship with God. Improving our education, reading widely, traveling broadly, being taught and mentored by the best and brightest, delving into the mysteries of life and nature—none of these offers the kind of wisdom that God provides us through the Holy Spirit.

Last, *cultivating a healthy and holy fear of the Lord gives us wisdom and understanding.* Our culture doesn't place much emphasis on fearing the Lord, but the Bible does!

Read Psalms 34:11; 111:10; Proverbs 8:13; 9:10; 16:6; and Matthew 10:28. According to these passages, what does it mean to fear the Lord?

Read Proverbs 8:12, 22–36. How is wisdom personified? Why do you think this is so?

How can you seek wisdom more fervently in your life? What steps can you take to recommit yourself to the things that matter?

Our search for wisdom ends with God. As we seek the Lord through prayer and the study of His Word, He instills His attributes in us. And when we identify ourselves with the person of Christ, we tap into His life-giving wisdom. Through Jesus, we can see life as God sees it, and we'll respond to life's challenges as we should.

The Passionate Testimony of
15 an Innocent Man
Selections from Job 29–31

> Let Him weigh me with accurate scales,
> And let God know my integrity.
>
> —Job 31:6

FORMER U.S. SENATOR ALAN SIMPSON once said, "If you have integrity, nothing else matters. If you *don't* have integrity, nothing else matters."[1] Unfortunately, in our culture, integrity seems to have fallen by the wayside. As personal and public trust has eroded, we've become guarded and suspicious of others. We've been hurt by the sins, betrayals, and failures of those we once trusted and respected. And we've been disappointed as well by our own failures in the area of personal integrity.

In contrast, Job clung to his integrity in every area of life. Maybe that explains why we regard him so highly. He was a man of integrity *before* the bottom fell out of his life, *when* it fell out of his life, and even *after* it fell out of his life—right up to the day he took his last breath. We admire his endurance in the face of excruciating suffering, but we stand in awe of the way he modeled integrity. Let's take a look at Job's life, as he described it. We'll note his close relationship with God, his favor among his peers, and his determination to live righteously.

TREASURES FROM THE TEXT

Job's Past Glory

In chapter 29, Job pined for his happy past as he reflected on his glory days. He longed to regain God's favor and feel His face shine on him once more.

And Job again took up his discourse and said,

"Oh that I were as in months gone by,
As in the days when God watched over me;
When His lamp shone over my head,
And by His light I walked through darkness;
As I was in the prime of my days,
When the friendship of God was over my tent;
When the Almighty was yet with me,
And my children were around me;
When my steps were bathed in butter,
And the rock poured out for me streams of oil!" (Job 29:1–6)

What images does Job use in this passage to illustrate the closeness of his relationship with God?

In Other Words

Job missed his close friendship with God even more than he missed his beloved children, servants, and flocks. Adam must have had similar feelings after the Fall. He may have thought, "How great it was when God and I walked in the cool of the evening, with no spiritual chasm separating us!" But Adam knew that his own sin had breached his relationship with the Lord. Job, on the other hand, hadn't a clue why God seemed to be turning His back on His servant.
One author writes,

Job had opened his defense by saying that he wished he had never been born (Job 3). Now he closed his defense by remembering the blessings he and his family had enjoyed prior to his crisis. This is a good reminder that we should try to see life in a balanced way. Yes, God permits us to experience difficulties and sorrows, but God also sends victories and joys. . . . C. H. Spurgeon said that too many people write their blessings in the sand but engrave their sorrows in marble. . . .

When we are experiencing trials, it's natural for us to long for "the good old days"; but our longing will not change our situation. Someone has defined "the good old days" as "a combination of a bad memory and a good imagination." In Job's case, however, his memory was accurate, and "the good old days" really were good.[2]

Like Adam and Job, we all look back nostalgically at special times in our lives. Maybe you felt more blessed, joyful, innocent, peaceful, passionate, or energetic at an earlier time in your life. Maybe you enjoyed good health and comfort before a physical illness reared its ugly head. Perhaps you felt extraordinarily blessed before a multitude of trials and disappointments crashed into your life. Or you may have experienced more satisfaction at the beginning of your marriage or at a previous stage in your family life. Maybe your early walk with the Lord seemed more fruitful than your current spiritual life. Do you find yourself wishing for the good old days?

List a special time or experience in your past that brings back good memories. What was so significant about this time?

Think of a creative "memorial" that you can set up to help you remember a specific instance when God worked in your life. What might it be?

Do you have a tendency to "write your blessings in the sand but engrave your sorrows in marble"? If so, list some ways that you can be more intentional about offering thanks for your blessings.

In the next section of chapter 29, Job described how he had once been greatly respected as a leader in Uz. Other people saw him as a man of integrity who was well respected for his wise counsel and kind treatment of others.

> When I went out to the gate of the city,
> When I took my seat in the square,
> The young men saw me and hid themselves,
> And the old men arose and stood.
> The princes stopped talking
> And put their hands on their mouths;
> The voice of the nobles was hushed,
> And their tongue stuck to their palate.
> For when the ear heard, it called me blessed,
> And when the eye saw, it gave witness of me,
> Because I delivered the poor who cried for help,
> And the orphan who had no helper. . . .
> I broke the jaws of the wicked
> And snatched the prey from his teeth. . . .
> I chose a way for them and sat as chief,
> And dwelt as a king among the troops,
> As one who comforted the mourners. (Job 29:7–12, 17, 25)

List several images from this passage that illustrate how much the townspeople respected Job. What is significant about these images?

In what ways did Job help the forsaken, hurting, and down-and-out in his community?

Instead of conducting himself haughtily and having a better-than-thou attitude, Job humbly served his friends and neighbors. He wisely and responsibly performed his duties as a community leader. He had been entrusted with great wealth, a large family, and an enormous estate, yet he didn't brag. Instead, he offered compassion to others, pouring his rich benevolences out to them like an offering of precious olive oil.

Job's Present Misery

In the next chapter, Job takes a sharp turn from describing his glorious past and begins to rehearse his present misery.

> But now those younger than I mock me,
> Whose fathers I disdained to put with the dogs of my flock. . . .
> And now I have become their taunt,
> I have even become a byword to them.
> They abhor me and stand aloof from me,
> And they do not refrain from spitting at my face. . . .
> Terrors are turned against me;
> They pursue my honor as the wind,
> And my prosperity has passed away like a cloud.
> And now my soul is poured out within me;
> Days of affliction have seized me.
> At night it pierces my bones within me,
> And my gnawing pains take no rest. (Job 30:1, 9–10, 15–17)

How does Job's present situation contrast with his past?

In what ways did the members of Job's community now look down upon him and mistreat him?

In the second half of chapter 30, Job turned his attention from his humiliation before men to his despair before God.

> I cry out to You for help, but You do not answer me;
> I stand up, and You turn Your attention against me. . . .
> Yet does not one in a heap of ruins stretch out his hand,
> Or in his disaster therefore cry out for help?
> Have I not wept for the one whose life is hard?
> Was not my soul grieved for the needy?
> When I expected good, then evil came;
> When I waited for light, then darkness came.
> I am seething within and cannot relax;
> Days of affliction confront me.
> I go about mourning without comfort;
> I stand up in the assembly and cry out for help. . . .
> My skin turns black on me,
> And my bones burn with fever.
> Therefore my harp is turned to mourning,
> And my flute to the sound of those who weep. (30:20, 24–28, 30–31)

Windows to the Ancient World

Job's grief and despair have turned his once-joyful song into a mournful tune. Several other Bible versions translate verse 31 as "my harp is *tuned* to mourning." Author Mike Mason writes:

Ancient music was not written in keys but in modes. There may have been no single standard for tuning instruments such as there is on a modern guitar or piano, but rather tuning could be altered to achieve a variety of musical effects. . . . In conventional western music the only modes that have been commonly preserved are the major and the minor; but ancient music featured a much broader and subtler modal palette. Modes were like moods. . . . Highly evocative, they bore a certain nostalgic correspondence to the changing weathers of the soul.

When Job said that his harp was "tuned to mourning," he meant that the circumstances of his life were such that all he could do was mourn. He could not produce any other kind of music, any more than a Mozart piano sonata could be played on the bagpipes.[3]

Job's grief-mode lament recalls this sad Psalm, a song with the heading "An Experience of the Captivity":

By the rivers of Babylon,
There we sat down and wept,
When we remembered Zion.
Upon the willows in the midst of it
We hung our harps.
For there our captors demanded of us songs,
And our tormenters mirth, saying,
"Sing us one of the songs of Zion."
How can we sing the LORD's song
In a foreign land? (Psalm 137:1–4)

This psalm records the grief of the Israelites who were captured and dragged away to Babylon in the sixth century BC, when the Babylonians besieged the city of Jerusalem. The city and much of the Judean countryside were plundered and destroyed. In addition, the Babylonians razed the temple and palace, and most of Israel's influential people were forcibly removed from their homes.[4]

Like Job, the Israelites found it difficult to offer praise to God in such horrible circumstances. Their once-lively songs of joy now turned to songs of mourning. Their hearts were heavy as their faith experienced such severe testing. Clearly, Job's heart was heavy from his trials, too. He couldn't fake joy when his soul overflowed with despair.

Job's Integrity

In chapter 31, Job made another rhetorical shift in his argument, affirming his innocence once more.

> I have made a covenant with my eyes;
> How then could I gaze at a virgin?
> And what is the portion of God from above
> Or the heritage of the Almighty from on high?
> Is it not calamity to the unjust
> And disaster to those who work iniquity?
> Does He not see my ways
> And number all my steps?
> If I have walked with falsehood,
> And my foot has hastened after deceit,
> Let Him weigh me with accurate scales,
> And let God know my integrity. . . .
> If my heart has been enticed by a woman,
> Or I have lurked at my neighbor's doorway,
> May my wife grind for another. . . .
> For that would be a lustful crime;
> Moreover, it would be an iniquity punishable by judges. (Job 31:1–6, 9–11)

Here, Job specifically asserted his blamelessness when it came to the sins of covetousness and lust. He reaffirmed his commitment to his wife and declared that he had not looked lustfully at young women. Next he expounded on his generous, fair treatment of his servants, noting that he had not abused his position of power over them:

> If I have despised the claim of my male or female slaves
> When they filed a complaint against me,
> What then could I do when God arises?
> And when He calls me to account, what will I answer Him?
> Did not He who made me in the womb make him,
> And the same one fashion us in the womb?
> If I have kept the poor from their desire,
> Or have caused the eyes of the widow to fail,
> Or have eaten my morsel alone,
> And the orphan has not shared it
> (But from my youth he grew up with me as with a father,
> And from infancy I guided her),
> If I have seen anyone perish for lack of clothing,
> Or that the needy had no covering,
> If his loins have not thanked me,
> And if he has not been warmed with the fleece of my sheep,
> If I have lifted up my hand against the orphan,
> Because I saw I had support in the gate,
> Let my shoulder fall from the socket,
> And my arm be broken off at the elbow. (Job 31:13–22)

Not only had Job treated his wife with dignity and respect, he had honored his servants and treated them fairly. In addition, he had generously provided food, clothing, and shelter for the poor. He'd given support to the widows in his community, and perhaps his most unselfish gift of all had been the provision of a father's love, support, and encouragement to orphaned girls and boys. So he wondered why he had received this painful "reward" for all the good deeds he had done.

Have I covered my transgressions like Adam,
By hiding my iniquity in my bosom,
Because I feared the great multitude,
And the contempt of families terrified me,
And kept silent and did not go out of doors?
Oh that I had one to hear me!
Behold, here is my signature;
Let the Almighty answer me!
And the indictment which my adversary has written,
Surely I would carry it on my shoulder,
I would bind it to myself like a crown.
I would declare to Him the number of my steps;
Like a prince I would approach Him. (Job 31:33–37)

Job cried out that, unlike Adam, he had not sinned against God. He again used judicial terms to describe his longing for a chance to appear in God's court and address the injustice he had received from the Lord. He openly demanded that his innocence be declared before God, his accusers, and the whole world.

NUGGETS OF WISDOM

From Job's testimony in these three chapters, we find three principles to apply to our own lives.

1. *Reflecting on our past blessings gives us reasons to rejoice.* Do this often! Mealtimes and bedtime present incredible opportunities to give thanks and to teach your children to do the same. Psalm 103 contains a beautifully expressive guideline for thanksgiving. It reads:

Bless the LORD, O my soul,
And all that is within me, bless His holy name.
Bless the LORD, O my soul,
And forget none of His benefits;
Who pardons all your iniquities,

Who heals all your diseases;
Who redeems your life from the pit,
Who crowns you with lovingkindness and compassion;
Who satisfies your years with good things,
So that your youth is renewed like the eagle. . . .
For as high as the heavens are above the earth,
So great is His lovingkindness toward those who fear Him.
As far as the east is from the west,
So far has He removed our transgressions from us. (103:1–5, 11–12)

2. *Rehearsing our present trials forces us to swallow our pride.* The apostle Paul experienced suffering precisely to keep him humble so that he could better glorify God. Paul wrote:

Because of the surpassing greatness of the revelations, for this reason, to keep me from exalting myself, there was given me a thorn in the flesh, a messenger of Satan to torment me—to keep me from exalting myself! Concerning this I implored the Lord three times that it might leave me. And He has said to me, "My grace is sufficient for you, for power is perfected in weakness." Most gladly, therefore, I will rather boast about my weaknesses, so that the power of Christ may dwell in me. (2 Corinthians 12:7–9)

As we drop our pride and cynicism, we're aligned with God's desires for us. Like Job's and Paul's struggles, our trials teach us to walk in humility and help us to empathize with others' pain.

3. *Reaffirming our commitment to integrity strengthens us with confidence and courage.* Job may have been troubled and discouraged, but he wasn't defeated. He wasn't haughty, but he stood his ground when it came to defending his integrity. He had the confidence to tell God, "If I have done anything worth this kind of punishment, then strike me dead right now!" But he hadn't, and God didn't.

Take some time now to think about the areas of your life in which your integrity faces the most challenges or resistance. What are these areas?

What people or activities provide encouragement and accountability for you in the area of personal integrity?

While Job fought a difficult battle against the false accusations of misguided people, Jesus Christ fought an even more intense one. The only truly innocent man, Jesus suffered an excruciating death on the cross for crimes that He had not committed. Yet He responded in love, even asking His Father to forgive His tormentors. Jesus trusted His Father to act as His just Judge and to vindicate Him, revealing the truth of Christ's Sonship to all mankind. And we'll soon see that God also vindicated Job, ending His silence and revealing Job's blamelessness to all.

16 Another Long-Winded Monologue
Selections from Job 32–37

> Listen to me, you men of understanding.
> Far be it from God to do wickedness,
> And from the Almighty to do wrong.
>
> —Job 34:10

EVER WATCHED ONE OF AMERICA'S presidential nominating conventions on TV? Just when you think you can't possibly listen to one more word, another speaker ascends to the podium. These speeches are the modern-day equivalent to the long-winded discourse of Job's friends!

In chapter 32, as if Job hadn't already heard enough from Eliphaz, Bildad, and Zophar, another friend named Elihu stepped up to offer his perspective on Job's situation. Elihu provided part true wisdom, part error, part set-up for the book's climactic ending, and part comic relief—if you can see the humor in taking two chapters' worth of ideas and expanding them into six!

And just who was this fuming friend, come to put a new face on Job's agony? He was the son of Barachel the Buzite, a descendant of Abraham's nephew Buz and a leading figure in a clan closely related to Job's. Elihu's name meant "He is my God," and it was a moniker that endured for years in Israelite families and appears several more times in the Bible (see 1 Samuel 1:1; 1 Chronicles 12:20; 26:7; 27:18). Elihu was much younger than Job and his three friends (Job 32:6), a fact that caused him to hold his tongue until now (32:4). He also may have been less known in the area than the others, since the book provides his full pedigree (32:2).

In Job 32–37, Elihu gave four speeches in which he attempted to explain the character of God and how it applied to Job's situation. While Elihu made some of the same points as Job's other friends, he had a different purpose. Instead of trying to prove that Job was guilty of unconfessed sin, he attempted to demonstrate that Job had a wrong view of God.

In Other Words

In his book *The Message of Job,* David Atkinson adds these insights:

Elihu opens up the theme of wisdom, which is a theological bridge in the story between Job's experience and his hearing the Lord. This will prove to be the theological significance of Elihu. But there is perhaps a dramatic purpose as well. These chapters give us a space between Job and Yahweh. They illustrate, just by being there, that Yahweh is not forced into a quick reply by the intensity of Job's entreaties. God acts in his own time; he is not at human beck and call. He "comes down his own secret stair," and in sovereign and gracious care, he decides the timing of his interventions. Elihu gives us this place to pause, and so serves the author's purpose of displaying the freedom of God. Elihu blusters away, he makes his own mistakes. But in the middle of his blusterings, there are some gems, and it is these gems which are part of the preparation Job needs—and we the readers need—to be ready to hear the Lord.[1]

Let's dig into the text to discover the "gems" that Elihu has to offer us.

TREASURES FROM THE TEXT

For twenty-nine chapters, Elihu waited patiently, listening to his elders—Job and his friends—debate. The three friends stood firm in their accusations; Job held to his innocence. Finally, Elihu couldn't take it any more. Hopping mad about what he had heard, he was about to erupt. An interlude of the book's only narrative prose, apart from its introduction and conclusion, sets the scene:

Then these three men ceased answering Job, because he was righteous in his own eyes. But the anger of Elihu the son of Barachel the Buzite, of the family of Ram burned; against Job his anger burned because he justified himself before God. And his anger burned against his three friends because they had found no answer, and yet had condemned Job. Now Elihu had waited to speak to Job because they were years older than he. And when Elihu saw that there was no answer in the mouth of the three men his anger burned. (Job 32:1–5)

Elihu resembles a new, young Christian with just enough experience and Bible knowledge to be dangerous. He knows enough to get his theology right sometimes, but not as often as he thinks. He brazenly begins his speech.

> So Elihu the son of Barachel the Buzite spoke out and said,
>   "I am young in years and you are old;
>   Therefore I was shy and afraid to tell you what I think. . . .
>   The abundant in years may not be wise,
>   Nor may elders understand justice.
>   So I say, 'Listen to me,
>   I too will tell what I think.'. . .
>   I too will answer my share,
>   I also will tell my opinion.
>   For I am full of words." (Job 32:6, 9, 17–18)

He said it! As we read on, we'll see that Elihu certainly was "full of words." He chose not to speak until the others had spoken, thus showing deference to his elders; however, he also noted that their old age did not necessarily guarantee a windfall of wisdom. Instead, he said, "The breath of the Almighty gives . . . understanding" (Job 32:8). Elihu had listened to the other friends, and he felt that they had no solid answers. He was convinced that his own wisdom from God would shed light on the situation. David Atkinson writes,

> Elihu is rather an enigma. He blusters on to the stage as an angry young man, full of his own importance, offering to clarify the situation for Job and his friends, angry with the muddle they have got themselves into. In one respect it is rather like a comic turn, for he manages to spend a lot of time not saying very much.[2]

Elihu's Four Mistakes

Elihu stumbled upon some good theology in his diatribe, but he made four obvious mistakes in his presentation.

1. *He took too long getting started.* Instead of quickly getting to the point, he rambled endlessly. All the while, suffering Job is forced to listen to this friend's long-winded soliloquy.

2. *Elihu came across as pompous.* Dogmatic and opinionated, he saw himself as the final authority, and he didn't welcome discussion or feedback from his audience—even from Job, who could teach him a thing or two. In fact, neither Job nor his three other friends interrupted his preaching or tried to answer him at any point—perhaps because Elihu was so angry. Who could get a word in edgewise? When he finally asked Job to respond (Job 34:33), Job remained silent. He'd heard most of this from his other friends and answered them; no further response was needed.

3. *He stated what Job already knew.* Elihu spent most of his time sharing his own ideas about God, mankind, wisdom, and justice. But he offered Job nothing new. What Job needed was a fresh perspective on his suffering. He longed for God to vindicate him, but until then, he could use a real friend—someone to encourage him to cling to his faith despite all odds.

4. *Elihu didn't leave room for mystery.* He never acknowledged that he didn't have all the answers. Instead of being teachable, he saw himself as the teacher and Job as his student. He said,

> Behold, let me tell you, you are not right in this,
> For God is greater than man.
> Why do you complain against Him
> That He does not give an account of all His doings?
> Indeed God speaks once,
> Or twice, yet no one notices it. . . .
> Pay attention, O Job, listen to me;
> Keep silent, and let me speak. (Job 33:12–14, 31)

Elihu's Four Speeches

Despite his shortcomings as a preacher, Elihu's speech did indeed give some insight into Job's situation. Elihu's primary emphasis was a positive one: focusing Job's attention (and ours) on the absolute sovereignty of God. Four speeches support this theme: the first in chapters 32 and 33, the second in 34, the third in 35, and the fourth in 36 and 37.

Elihu's first speech suggests that God has not been silent. Rather, he noted in verses 13 and 14 listed above that Yahweh had been speaking, but just not as Job expected. First of all, Elihu asserted, *God speaks through dreams and visions.*

> In a dream, a vision of the night,
> When sound sleep falls on men,
> While they slumber in their beds,
> Then He opens the ears of men,
> And seals their instruction. (Job 33:15–16)

In addition, in a significant insight into the sovereignty of God, Elihu said that *God speaks through suffering:*

> Man is also chastened with pain on his bed,
> And with unceasing complaint in his bones;
> So that his life loathes bread,
> And his soul favorite food.
> His flesh wastes away from sight,
> And his bones which were not seen stick out.
> Then his soul draws near to the pit,
> And his life to those who bring death. (Job 33:19–22)

The result of such chastening is actually given in the two previous verses:

> That He may turn man aside from his conduct,
> And keep man from pride;
> He keeps back his soul from the pit. (Job 33:17–18)

In his book *The Problem of Pain,* C. S. Lewis wrote: "God whispers to us in our pleasures, speaks in our conscience, but shouts in our pains: it is His megaphone to rouse a deaf world."[3] God can use pain to teach us, warn us, humble us, and bring us into submission to His will. Often, God disciplines a person to turn him from error. In addition, suffering can actually be a way to keep us from committing certain sins. It can soften our hearts and teach us to depend on Him.

Think of a time that God used pain to teach you something. What were the circumstances?

How did God use this situation constructively in your life?

Next, Elihu suggested that *God may also speak through the ministry of a special mediating angel:*

> If there is an angel as mediator for him,
> One out of a thousand,
> To remind a man what is right for him,
> Then let him be gracious to him, and say,
> "Deliver him from going down to the pit,
> I have found a ransom";
> Let his flesh become fresher than in youth,
> Let him return to the days of his youthful vigor;
> Then he will pray to God, and He will accept him,
> That he may see His face with joy,
> And He may restore His righteousness to man. (Job 33:23–26)

Angels are mentioned several times in the book of Job, but this mediating angel is a source of divine information that has not yet been addressed. Warren Wiersbe suggests:

> It seems likely that this interceding angel is the Angel of the Lord, our Lord Jesus Christ, the Mediator who gave His life as a ransom for sinners (1 Tim. 2:5; Mark 10:45). As the Angel of the Lord, the Son of God visited the earth in Old Testament times to deliver special messages and accomplish important tasks (Gen. 16:9; 22:11; Ex. 3:2; Jud. 6:11). But Elihu saw this angel not only as a mediator between God and men, but also as the provider of the ransom of sinners. *This is the heavenly "mediator" that Job has been asking for throughout the debate!* [4]

In what ways has Christ acted as our mediator? What is the significance of these acts?

In his second speech, after alleging Job's wickedness (Job 34:7–9), Elihu proclaimed the sovereignty of God—that He governs justly, without exception.

> Therefore, listen to me, you men of understanding.
> Far be it from God to do wickedness,
> And from the Almighty to do wrong.
> For He pays a man according to his work,
> And makes him find it according to his way.
> Surely, God will not act wickedly,
> And the Almighty will not pervert justice.
> Who gave Him authority over the earth?
> And who has laid on Him the whole world?
> If He should determine to do so,
> If He should gather to Himself His spirit and His breath,
> All flesh would perish together,
> And man would return to dust. (Job 34:10–15)

Elihu stressed that God is fair, He is good, and He has His own divine purpose for every event that occurs in our lives. God is never shocked or surprised. He never loses control of His creation. And furthermore, He's not obligated to explain Himself.

In his third speech, Elihu accused Job of claiming to be sinless (Job 35:1–3). However, Job (and God) have said that Job is *blameless,* not sinless. Elihu suggested that Yahweh would not listen to Job unless he would confesses his wrongdoing:

> Surely God will not listen to an empty cry,
> Nor will the Almighty regard it.
> How much less when you say you do not behold Him,
> The case is before Him, and you must wait for Him!
> And now, because He has not visited in His anger,
> Nor has He acknowledged transgression well,
> So Job opens his mouth emptily;
> He multiplies words without knowledge. (Job 35:13–16)

What would you say is the difference between being *blameless* and being *sinless?*

According to the opening chapters of Job, how did Job atone for his sin?

Although long-winded and misguided in his assessment of Job, Elihu concluded his speeches with a marvelous declaration of God's majesty and His faithfulness to the righteous:

> Listen to this, O Job,
> Stand and consider the wonders of God.
> Do you know how God establishes them,
> And makes the lightening of His cloud to shine?

> Do you know about the layers of the thick clouds,
> The wonders of one perfect in knowledge . . . ?
> Can you, with Him, spread out the skies . . . ?
> Out of the north comes golden splendor;
> Around God is awesome majesty.
> The Almighty—we cannot find Him;
> He is exalted in power;
> And He will not do violence to justice and abundant righteousness. (Job 37:14–16, 18, 22–23)

Some of Elihu's ideas may have been incorrect, but when it came to describing the Lord's omnipotence and magnificence, he *got it!* Our God is transcendent. He's magnificent. He's mighty. He's gigantic! And without Him, there's no righteousness. There's no holiness. There's no ability to change. There's no truth. God authors it all.

Elihu came to terms with these marvelous truths as he described the awesome power of a thunderstorm.

> At this also my heart trembles,
> And leaps from its place.
> Listen closely to the thunder of His voice,
> And the rumbling that goes out from His mouth.
> Under the whole heaven He lets it loose,
> And His lightning to the ends of the earth. . . .
> God thunders with His voice wondrously,
> Doing great things which we cannot comprehend. (Job 37:1–3, 5)

Essentially, he told Job, "If God's big enough to handle all the mysteries of creation, He's big enough to handle all of your problems, all of your suffering, and even all of your questions."

What problems or difficult situations are you experiencing in your life right now? Are you trusting God to help you solve them, or are you seeking solutions on your own?

What questions do you have for God right now?

What steps can you take to release the things you're holding on to and place them in God's hands?

NUGGETS OF WISDOM

When our minds conceive of God as "too small," our problems are magnified. We tend to retreat in fear and insecurity. The first three friends to speak considered God to be too small to handle all of the suffering and all of the questions Job threw His way.

However, when we recognize the "bigness" of our God, our problems seem more insignificant. We gain a correct perspective on our lives. We choose to stand in awe and worship Him. Thankfully, Job knew he served a big God—a mighty, powerful, and sovereign God. Job knew that he could wrestle with the mysteries of God and still not diminish Yahweh's character or power in any way.

The question for you, then, is a simple one: How big is your God? Big enough to intervene in your life? Big enough to heal your past wounds? Big enough for you to hold Him in awe? Big enough for you to offer Him your ultimate trust and respect? Big enough to handle all of your pain and all of your worries? Big enough to love you unconditionally despite your sin and your failures? Big enough to comfort you and restore you to a right relationship with Him?

Read Matthew 6:33–34. Often, worry is an indication that we've let our concept of God get too small. The Bible says we have a heavenly Provider (Genesis 22:14;), Healer (Psalm 147:3; Luke 4:40), Creator (Genesis 2; Isaiah 43:1), Redeemer (Galatians 3:13–14; Titus 2:13–14), and Friend (John 15:15). He can handle whatever you toss His way.

What areas have you been holding on to that you need to surrender to Him?

Take time now to write out a prayer of worship and thanksgiving to God for who He is and all the ways He has provided for your needs.

Don't forget—He's big enough to care for His entire creation. He fashioned this world, set the earth, stars, and planets in motion, and knew you intimately before you were even born. As your loving, powerful heavenly Father, He's uniquely equipped to handle anything that comes your way!

17 *A Penetrating Reproof from the Almighty*

Selections from Job 38:1–40:5

> **Where were you when I laid the foundation of the earth?**
>
> **Tell Me, if you have understanding,**
>
> **Who sets its measurements? Since you know.**
>
> —Job 38:4–5

GOD OFTEN CONNECTS with us in a most unusual way. And when He does, He often says the most unexpected things!

In July 1505, young Martin Luther committed his life to Christian service in the midst of a violent thunderstorm. The thunder and lightning so frightened him that "he fell to the earth and tremblingly exclaimed: 'Help, beloved Saint Anna! I will become a monk.'"[1] He held to that promise and flung himself on the altar of religious duty, entering the Augustinian monastery in Erfurt, Germany. He later said, "If ever a monk got to heaven by monkery, I would have gotten there."[2] According to the church's standards, he appeared blameless. Yet, despite endless confession and penance, he could not escape the feelings of guilt and despair that washed over his soul.

One day Luther's mentor, Johannes von Staupitz, offered the young man a sliver of hope. This friend encouraged Luther to study Scripture for himself, focusing on the person of Christ, the Cross, and the believer's righteousness obtained by faith. As Luther began to study the Scriptures, particularly Paul's letter to the Romans, God's revelation struck him like a lightning bolt:

> For I am not ashamed of the gospel, for it is the power of God for salvation to everyone who believes, to the Jew first and also to the Greek. For in it the righteousness of God is revealed from faith to faith; as it is written, "But the righteous man shall live by faith." (Romans 1:16–17)

Most of us were raised to think that God always speaks in a still, small voice in our inner being, whispering to us in a calm, peaceful setting. We assume His tone will be gentle, like the voice the boy Samuel heard from his bed in the temple and the prophet Elijah heard at the mouth of the cave at Horeb. But that's not always true! There are times when God must use a storm to get our attention in the midst of our chaotic lives. The prophet Nahum wrote:

> The Lord is slow to anger and great in power. . . .
> In whirlwind and storm is His way,
> And clouds are the dust beneath His feet. (Nahum 1:3)

Just as a thunderstorm marked an important turning point in Luther's spiritual journey, Job's pilgrimage of suffering came full circle when God revealed Himself through a powerful storm.

For Job, God had been silent for thirty-seven chapters, but now, the time had finally come for Him to speak. And when He did, He didn't just whisper, "Psst, Job! It's Me . . . God." Instead, He appeared on the scene and thundered in a whirlwind of fiery intensity.

TREASURES FROM THE TEXT

God's Reproof

Once God broke the silence, you'll be surprised to discover what He did *not* do. He didn't give Job any answers to his questions. He didn't apologize for having been silent so long. He didn't offer a hint of information about the whole thing between Himself and Satan way back when it all started. Furthermore, God didn't acknowledge that Job had been through deep struggles. When He finally spoke, He began with a reproof.

God's thundering address centered on His magnificent works in nature. Believe it or not, He asked *seventy-seven questions,* interspersed with His own divine commentary. God's response forced Job to recognize his own inadequacy and his inability to meet the Almighty on equal terms.

Warren Wiersbe writes,

> God is now called "the Lord," that is, [Yahweh], a name that (except for 12:9) has
> not been used in the Book of Job since the first two chapters. In their speeches, the

men have called Him "God" and "the Almighty" but not "[Yahweh]." This is the name that God revealed to Israel centuries later (Ex. 3:13ff), the name that speaks of His self-existence ("I AM THAT I AM") and His personal covenant relationship to His people.[3]

God's Intimate Knowledge of Creation

Once God got Job's attention, He gave two "speeches." His first is recorded in Job 38:1–40:5. His second begins at Job 40:6. Yahweh's address in chapters 38 though 42 can be summarized in two sets of questions.

First, God asks, *Can you explain or control My creation?* (Job 38:1–40:2). This first set of questions deals with Job's intellectual inadequacy. In the next set (Job 40:6–41:34), God reminds Job of his physical inadequacy by asking *Can you change or subdue my creation?* The first set of questions will be addressed in this chapter, the second set in chapter 18 of this guide.

The Almighty began by describing the extraordinary wisdom He used to create the world.

> Then the LORD answered Job out of the whirlwind and said,
> "Who is this that darkens counsel
> By words without knowledge?
> Now gird up your loins like a man,
> And I will ask you, and you instruct Me!
> Where were you when I laid the foundation of the earth?
> Tell Me, if you have understanding,
> Who set its measurements? Since you know.
> Or who stretched the line on it?
> On what were its bases sunk?
> Or who laid its cornerstone,
> When the morning stars sang together
> And all the sons of God shouted for joy?" (Job 38:1–7)

God's response was not meant to be cruel, but it *was* meant to stop Job in his tracks. Job needed a refresher course on Who's in charge. He needed to realize that God's ways and works are beyond our ability to understand. Keep in mind that there was not a whole group of people standing here; it was just Job and God. So the "Who's in charge" question had a pretty simple answer!

Which images from this passage stand out to you most clearly? What is so vivid about them?

How do God's words change your perspective on Job's situation?

God, the Master Architect, perfectly measured and planned everything that He created. Not a single mistake was made. In fact, the finished product was so glorious that the "morning stars sang together" and the angels shouted for joy!

Next, God described the exacting detail with which He measured and filled the powerful seas:

> Or who enclosed the sea with doors
> When, bursting forth, it went out from the womb;
> When I made a cloud its garment
> And thick darkness its swaddling band,
> And I placed boundaries on it
> And set a bolt and doors,
> And I said, "Thus far you shall come, but no farther;
> And here shall your proud waves stop"? (Job 38:8–11)

Yahweh used rich imagery to describe the painstaking way He set the oceans' boundaries. Then He illustrated the way in which He created the sun and moon, commanding the heavenly host like troops going into battle:

> Have you ever in your life commanded the morning,
> And caused the dawn to know its place,
> That it might take hold of the ends of the earth,
> And the wicked be shaken out of it? . . .

> Have you entered into the springs of the sea
> Or walked in the recesses of the deep?
> Have the gates of death been revealed to you,
> Or have you seen the gates of deep darkness?
> Have you understood the expanse of the earth?
> Tell Me, if you know all this. (Job 38:12–13, 16–18)

God described the sun's light at dawn spreading across the world, revealing the details of the earth's beautiful landscape. The daylight also exposes evil deeds that have been done in the darkness, and it keeps criminals from committing more wickedness.

Next, the Almighty asked Job if he could explain or if he had any control over the precipitation that falls during the various seasons.

> Have you entered the storehouses of the snow,
> Or have you seen the storehouses of the hail,
> Which I have reserved for the time of distress,
> For the day of war and battle? . . .
> Can you bind the chains of the Pleiades,
> Or loose the cords of Orion?
> Can you lead forth a constellation in its season,
> And guide the Bear with her satellites?
> Do you know the ordinances of the heavens,
> Or fix their rule over the earth? (Job 38:22–23, 31–33)

By this time, Job had probably had enough, but the Lord kept right on speaking! He focused Job's attention on the constellations in the heavens. Job couldn't fully understand the laws that govern their movements, nor could he control the stars and planets.

Similarly, in verses 34 through 38, the Lord called Job's attention to the clouds. Could Job order the clouds to drop rain on the earth below? Was the lightning a soldier under Job's command, reporting for duty? Of course not. God's words were full of irony, but that's what Job needed to rein in his pride, bring him back down to earth, and keep him from demanding so much.

Having detailed the heavens, God continued by asking Job questions about the intricate, mysterious animal kingdom He created.

Do you know the time the mountain goats give birth?
Do you observe the calving of the deer? . . .
Who sent out the wild donkey free?
And who loosed the bonds of the swift donkey? . . .
Will the wild ox consent to serve you,
Or will he spend the night at your manger? . . .
Do you give the horse his might?
Do you clothe his neck with a mane? . . .
Is it by your understanding that the hawk soars,
Stretching his wings toward the south?
Is it at your command that the eagle mounts up
And makes his nest on high?" (Job 39:1, 5, 9, 19, 26–27)

What point do you think God was making by referring to these animals?

Job's Response

Finally, in chapter 40, God responded to Job's urgent cry for the opportunity to defend himself against the Almighty. But what He said was probably not the answer that Job had in mind. The Lord said,

> Will the faultfinder contend with the Almighty?
> Let him who reproves God answer it. (Job 40:2)

Strong words! Yahweh had presented His case; now it was Job's turn to present his. But, when faced with the Almighty God, all of Job's lofty words and well-practiced arguments escaped him. All he could do was fall onto his face before the Lord and say:

> Behold, I am insignificant; what can I reply to You?
> I lay my hand on my mouth.
> Once I have spoken, and I will not answer;
> Even twice, and I will add nothing more. (Job 40:4–5)

Job didn't get what he thought he wanted, but he got what he *needed*. Instead of hearing more empty postulations, false assumptions, misguided explanations, and useless arguments, he finally heard God speak. In the lingering silence that followed, he recognized at last the sovereignty of the Almighty.

When have you sensed God speaking to you in a "storm" (a difficult situation)? What did He say?

What did He teach you through this experience?

NUGGETS OF WISDOM

As we examine Job's response carefully, we find three statements with special meaning for our lives.

1. *"I am insignificant."* Modern psychology has taught us just the opposite! We've been encouraged to recognize our value, importance, and significance as people, and there's certainly a place for recognizing our worth. But when we come face to face with the Living God, we quickly realize that we're nothing without Him.

Notice that God didn't reprove Job for saying, "I am insignificant." Clearly, the Almighty meant for Job to stand in quiet awe of His power and might. Job's statement was one of needed humility.

2. *"What can I reply?"* Suddenly, all his petty questions and demands meant very little. God didn't want answers; He knew the answers. If Job couldn't explain the inner workings of nature, how could he explain or understand his own situation? Yet God offered Job relief from his mental anguish by saying, "Rest in Me. Trust Me. I can handle it all."

3. *"I lay my hand on my mouth."* Job had ordered his friends to do this when they spoke harsh and unkind words. Now, it was time for him to swallow a spoonful of his own medicine. In the face of God's power, sovereignty, and grace, nothing Job said would have made any difference. So he surrendered to the majesty of the Almighty.

Taking Truth to Heart

From these three statements, we can glean three principles to apply to our lives.

- Since God's ways are higher than mine, then whatever He allows . . . I bow in submission. And that humbles me.
- Since God is in full control, then however He directs my steps . . . I follow in obedience. And that relieves me.
- Since God has the answers I lack, then whenever He speaks . . . I listen in silence. And that instructs me.

We are not by nature humble, submissive, or quiet. We like to be in charge. We seek to be in control. We like calling the shots. Many times, we don't like surprises—even God's surprises. Nor do we like having to wait for His answer, especially in complete stillness and silence. We'd rather seek forgiveness than permission. We'd rather resist than obey. We'd rather talk than listen. And we'd much rather take charge than submit.

When we learn to let go, however, God speaks. He may send storms our way to get our attention, but He then moves in radical ways to fine-tune our lives and get our spiritual motors running again. He offers love, grace, and provision if we will simply give up our own selfish plans and motives and allow Him to take control of our lives.

The book of Job teaches us that our response to life is a choice. Our attitude is a choice. And, if it takes a walk through the zoo like the one Job took to understand this truth, we should take that walk! When we look at the magnitude of God, we see how insignificant a lot of our personal preferences are. We plan our life one way; God plans it another. When we decide to cooperate with Him, everyone will notice!

In Other Words

One author describes how his marriage changed when he put the principles listed above into practice.

I made a vow to myself on the drive down to the vacation beach cottage. For two weeks I would try to be a loving husband and father. Totally loving. No ifs, ands, or buts. The idea had come to me as I listened to a commentator on my car's tape player. He was quoting a biblical passage about husbands being thoughtful of their wives. Then he went on to say, "Love is an act of the will. A person can choose to love." To myself, I had to admit that I had been a selfish husband—that our love had been dulled by my own insensitivity. In petty ways, really: chiding Evelyn for her tardiness; insisting on the TV channel I wanted to watch; throwing out day-old newspapers before Evelyn had a chance to read them. Well, for two weeks all that would change.

And it did. Right from the moment I kissed Evelyn at the door and said, "That new yellow sweater looks great on you."

"Oh, Tom, you noticed," she said, surprised and pleased. And maybe a little shocked.

After the long drive, I wanted to sit and read. Evelyn suggested a walk on the beach. I started to refuse, but then I thought, Evelyn's been alone here with the kids all week and now she wants to be alone with me. We walked on the beach while the children flew their kites.

So it went. Two weeks of not calling the Wall Street investment firm where I am a director; a visit to the shell museum, though I usually hate museums; holding my tongue while Evelyn's getting ready made us late for a dinner date. Relaxed and happy, that's how the whole vacation passed. I made a new vow to keep on remembering to choose love.

There was one thing that went wrong with my experiment, however. On the last night at our cottage, preparing for bed, Evelyn stared at me with the saddest expression.

"What's the matter?" I asked her.

"Tom," she said, in a voice filled with distress, "do you know something I don't?"

"What do you mean?"

"Well . . . that checkup I had several weeks ago . . . our doctor . . . did he tell you something about me? Tom, you've been so good to me . . . am I dying?"

It took a moment for it all to sink in. Then I burst out laughing. "No, honey," I said, wrapping her in my arms, "you're not dying; I'm just starting to live!"[4]

What do you learn about submission to God's will and obedience to His ways through this story? Through Job's story?

Which relationships in your life are suffering due to a lack of unselfish love, attention, motivation, creativity, or connection? What can you do to rekindle the flame?

Read Galatians 5:22–23. Think about how God has used difficult situations to cultivate the fruit of the Spirit in your life. In what ways do you currently demonstrate the fruit of the Spirit to others?

What steps can you take to enhance your ability to walk by the Spirit and see Him manifest more fruit in your life?

When God finally spoke to Job, the words probably weren't what Job had expected. But the Lord's sharp reproof got Job's mind off his own suffering and provided him with a new perspective on his God, his life, and even his personal pain. He looked around and discovered that the exquisite world that God had created still existed, and the Almighty was still in charge.

18 Full Repentance for All the Right Reasons

Selections from Job 40:6–42:6

> Therefore I retract,
> And I repent in dust and ashes.
>
> —Job 42:6

Iт's DIFFICULT TO CULTIVATE A HUMBLE HEART in our contentious culture. When was the last time you heard the words, "I'm sorry; I was wrong. Will you please forgive me?"

For most of us, it's been a while. And perhaps it's been a while since we've spoken these relationship-mending, soul-soothing words to someone else, too. Why do we so rarely hear (or give) such a contrite, honest confession? Because all of us have sinful natures that are given to pride and self-protection. It's tough to maintain an attitude of humility and graciousness in our "me-first" culture.

Now, let's try something else that's rare: starting at the end of our Scripture passage rather than at the beginning. Job 42:6, the last verse discussed in this study guide chapter, contains the beautiful jewel of Job's confession before God. As you study it in more detail, remember that this is what resulted from God's questions.

> Therefore I retract,
> And I repent in dust and ashes. (Job 42:6)

As this "jewel of repentance" is examined more closely, you'll discover how the light of Job's honest, contrite confession can illuminate your own life.

191

TREASURES FROM THE TEXT

God's Questioning Continued

We've already seen that it's a powerful thing when God shows up! In chapter 40, He manifested His splendor and fearsome majesty as He continued to question Job from the midst of the whirlwind.

> Then the LORD answered Job out of the storm and said,
>> "Now gird up your loins like a man;
>> I will ask you, and you instruct Me.
>> Will you really annul My judgment?
>> Will you condemn Me that you may be justified?
>> Or do you have an arm like God,
>> And can you thunder with a voice like His?
>> Adorn yourself with eminence and dignity,
>> And clothe yourself with honor and majesty.
>> Pour out the overflowings of your anger,
>> And look on everyone who is proud, and make him low.
>> Look on everyone who is proud, and humble him,
>> And tread down the wicked where they stand.
>> Hide them in the dust together;
>> Bind them in the hidden place.
>> Then I will also confess to you,
>> That your own right hand can save you. (Job 40:6–14)

God checked Job's pride by asking him, "If you know so much, why don't you instruct Me? If you're so powerful, why don't you run the world for a while?" Naturally, Job knew that he couldn't, and he ultimately humbled himself before his Creator.

God's Ultimate Power over Creation

In Job 40:6–41:34, we come to God's second "speech" in which he asked Job, *"Can you change or subdue my creation?"* Instead of confronting Job again with the broad sweep of His creation, as we studied in the last chapter, God selected two creatures and asked Job to consider them. You may recall that Job had accused God of treating him unjustly and, in addition, of failing to punish the wicked. Here God demonstrates His supreme ability to administer justice by giving Job a display of His physical power. God told Job, in essence, "See if you can do better! Here are two of My finest, fiercest creatures. If you can subdue them, then *maybe* you'll be qualified to execute judgment against a sinful world."

First, God asked Job to consider the magnificent creature called *Behemoth:*

> Behold now, Behemoth, which I made as well as you;
> He eats grass like an ox.
> Behold now, his strength in his loins
> And his power in the muscles of his belly.
> He bends his tail like a cedar;
> The sinews of his thighs are knit together.
> His bones are tubes of bronze;
> His limbs are like bars of iron. . . .
> Surely the mountains bring him food,
> And all the beasts of the field play there.
> Under the lotus plants he lies down,
> In the covert of the reeds and the marsh. . . .
> If a river rages, he is not alarmed;
> He is confident, though the Jordan rushes to his mouth.
> Can anyone capture him when he is on watch,
> With barbs can anyone pierce his nose? (Job 40:15–18, 20–21, 22–24)

Getting to the Root

God offered quite a detailed description of this fearsome creature! The Hebrew word for Behemoth literally means "super-beast."

Most scholars believe that God was describing a hippopotamus. Others suggest that it may have been an elephant, a water buffalo, or even a mythological creature. Today's big-game hunters, with their modern weapons, may not fear these beasts, but these animals would have been formidable enemies in the days of bows and arrows, spears, and slingshots.

Author Mike Mason writes,

> Now we come to the final ring of the Lord's three-ring circus, the ring that contains (next to man) the grandest and most mysterious of all His creatures: Behemoth and Leviathan.
>
> We all know that when we go to the zoo we will see lions, tigers, bears, and elephants. But what if we heard about a zoo where we could see living dinosaurs? Or a zoo where wildness itself—the very spirit of savagery—had been caught in a cage and put on visible display for human eyes to inspect? Or what if all the most spectacular features of all the world's greatest animals had somehow been lumped together and combined into one magnificent beast? Wouldn't that be a sight worth seeing?
>
> Perhaps this is something of the effect the Lord intends by His description of the Behemoth.[1]

Next, God goes on to describe another awe-inspiring creature—*Leviathan*.

> Can you draw out Leviathan with a fishhook?
> Or press down his tongue with a cord?
> Can you put a rope in his nose
> Or pierce his jaw with a hook?
> Will he make many supplications to you,
> Or will he speak to you soft words? . . .
> Will you play with him as with a bird,
> Or will you bind him for your maidens? . . .
> Who can strip off his outer armor?
> Who can come within his double mail? . . .
> Out of his mouth go burning torches;
> Sparks of fire leap forth. . . .
> Nothing on earth is like him,

One made without fear.
He looks on everything that is high;
He is king over all the sons of pride. (Job 41:1–3, 5, 13, 19, 33–34)

Most scholars and commentators believe that the term *Leviathan* represents the crocodile. Again, however, the creature described here seems to have supernatural qualities and powers greater than those of an everyday crocodile. It's possible that God is using the word *Leviathan* to describe an otherworldly, apocalyptic, or mythical beast with supernatural strength and symbolic significance.

The description of Leviathan—with burning torches emanating from his mouth, smoke pouring out of his nostrils, and breath that can set coals ablaze—sounds more like the description of a fierce, fire-breathing dragon than of an ordinary crocodile. Some scholars draw a parallel between this dragon and Satan. Mike Mason writes,

> While it is true that Satan is never named outside the Prologue, this does not mean that the Lord never deals with him. He deals with him here in the form of Leviathan, describing him to Job with the same sort of symbolic picture-language He uses in *Revelation,* where the Devil is also portrayed as a great dragon who is to be "thrown into the Abyss" (20:2–3).[2]

What exactly were God's purposes in describing these two extraordinary creatures? One author writes this concerning God's description of these beasts:

> By telling of his dominion over Behemoth and Leviathan, the Lord is illustrating what he has said in 40:8–14. He is celebrating his moral triumph over the forces of evil. Satan, the Accuser, has been proved wrong, though Job does not know it. The author and the reader see the entire picture that Job and his friends never knew. God permitted the Accuser to touch Job as part of his plan to humiliate Satan. But now that the contest is over, God still did not reveal his reason to Job. Because Job did not find out what the readers know, he could be restored without destroying the integrity of the account. . . . If the specific and ultimate reason for his suffering had been revealed to Job . . . the value of the account as a comfort to others who must suffer in ignorance would have been diminished if not cancelled.[3]

God's extraordinary descriptions of these two larger-than-life creatures were all Job needed to hear. The suffering man humbly recognized his utter inability to understand or reign over God's vast creation. Even more important, he finally realized that he had falsely accused God of cruelty and injustice against him.

Job's confession, found in the first several verses of chapter 42, contains some of the richest truths in all of Scripture. Eugene Peterson renders the passage this way in *The Message*:

> Job answered GOD:
>   I'm convinced: You can do anything and everything.
>   Nothing and no one can upset your plans.
>   You asked, 'Who is this muddying the water,
>   ignorantly confusing the issue, second-guessing my purposes?'
>   I admit it. I was the one. I babbled on about things far beyond me,
>   made small talk about wonders way over my head.
>   You told me, 'Listen, and let me do the talking.
>   Let me ask the questions. *You* give the answers.'
>   I admit I once lived by rumors of you;
>   now I have it all firsthand—from my own eyes and ears!
>   I'm sorry—forgive me. I'll never do that again, I promise!
>   I'll never again live on crusts of hearsay, crumbs of rumor." (Job 42:1–5 MSG)

Job knew that he had lost the battle; he couldn't argue his case with God. He told the Almighty, in essence, "I can't answer your questions! All I can do now is confess that I spoke misguided, prideful words." Once he saw firsthand the glory of the Lord, Job immediately humbled himself, admitted he was wrong, and repented in dust and ashes.

What confessions did Job make in this passage?

In what ways do you think Job had lived on "crusts of hearsay" and "crumbs of rumor"?

When have you misjudged a person due to hearsay or rumor? What made you realize that you were incorrect in your assumptions?

Commentator John E. Hartley writes,

> Job has come to a true assessment of himself before the holy God. . . . Job both renounces all false pride and concedes that God has been true to justice in allowing him . . . to be brought so low that he has had to sit outside the city on the ash heap. The term *recant (niham)* means to turn from a planned course of action and take up a new course. It implies the strongest resolve to change direction."[4]

Incredibly, Job's suffering hadn't lessened at all, yet he still repented of his harsh words toward God. What can we learn from this?

Pastor Charles Haddon Spurgeon once wrote, "The door of repentance opens into the hall of joy."[5] How have you found this to be true?

Why does God require repentance and humility from us? What do we gain from having a humble, teachable spirit?

Nuggets of Wisdom

Job's words of repentance echoed years later in the life of another man, David. This anointed king of Israel had committed the sins of lust, adultery, deceit, and murder. Struggling under the crushing weight of his guilt, he finally reached rock bottom and cried out to God. In the poignant words of Psalm 51, David pours out his full confession with a repentant heart.

> Be gracious to me, O God, according to Your lovingkindness;
> According to the greatness of Your compassion blot out my transgressions.
> Wash me thoroughly from my iniquity
> And cleanse me from my sin.
> For I know my transgressions,
> And my sin is ever before me. . . .
> Create in me a clean heart, O God,
> And renew a steadfast spirit within me. . . .
> The sacrifices of God are a broken spirit;
> A broken and a contrite heart, O God, You will not despise.
> (Psalm 51:1–3, 10, 17)

When David confessed his sin and approached God with "a broken and a contrite heart," he finally received the Lord's gracious forgiveness and restoration. But what does it mean to possess a truly humble heart and a repentant spirit? Let's examine five vital characteristics of a contrite heart.

First, *a contrite heart nurses no grudges*. A contrite person takes responsibility for his or her own words and actions. She refuses to play the victim and doesn't blame others. Instead, a humble person asks for forgiveness, rights wrongs, and forgives others as well.

Second, *a contrite heart makes no demands.* A person with a truly repentant spirit doesn't say, "Listen, I'll make you a deal. If you do this, then I'll apologize." Instead, he offers a humble apology without demanding anything in return.

Third, *a contrite heart has no expectations.* A humble person doesn't expect the royal treatment, storming off in a huff of indignation if she doesn't receive it. A humble person doesn't tell others, "It's my way or the highway." A humble person doesn't demand forgiveness; she waits patiently for it. And even if reconciliation never occurs, a humble person continues to respond to others with grace.

Fourth, *a contrite heart offers no conditions.* A repentant person doesn't offer God or others any "ifs, ands, or buts." There's no leveraging, no deal making, no trying to make himself look good.

Fifth, *a contrite heart anticipates no favors.* A person who sees herself rightly before God will not have a hidden agenda. She won't demand, "If I forgive you for this, you have to forgive me for that" or "If you do this for me, then I'll forgive you." A humble person doesn't use forgiveness as a weapon to manipulate others.

Name a past situation in which you repented of your words or actions and asked God or another person for forgiveness. Did this act of repentance help reconcile your relationship? If so, how?

Is there anyone in your life to whom you owe an apology? If so, who is it, and why do you need to apologize?

What could you say to or do to show that you want to restore your relationship with this person?

Commit yourself to making contact with this person sometime this week. If possible, make an appointment, and stick to it! Even a simple phone call or e-mail can make an incredible difference in mending the threads of a torn relationship. When a relationship is strained or broken, both people feel pain and disappointment. When one person takes a step to mend that relationship, the other often responds with gratitude and grace.

There may be circumstances, however, in which it is impossible (as in a death), unsafe, or unwise to initiate contact. In these cases, seek to reconcile the hurt within your own heart and continue to prayerfully seek God's will for the situation. God promises to use you in remarkable ways when you approach Him and others with a humble heart.

Taking Truth to Heart

The following story illustrates the poignant lesson that caused one young man to repent:

Years ago, Cynthia and I were friends with a wonderful Christian family—a dad and mom and three sons. The oldest son was greatly gifted intellectually and musically. Earlier in his high school years, the father had some trouble with the boy's spirit of submission. A proud streak accompanied the boy's independent spirit.

Upon graduating from high school, the boy began his first year of college many miles from home. It wasn't long before he started running with a tough crowd and picked up a surly, rebellious spirit. After completing his freshman year, he returned home, bringing his proud independence with him. His arrogant, stubborn, and mean-spirited attitude disrupted the harmony of his family. Late one afternoon, his father had finally had enough.

He called the boy into his study and said firmly, "Sit down." He then delivered a speech the boy would never forget. "Everything you have is mine. I bought every stitch of clothing you wear and everything that hangs in your closet. Your car out there in the driveway is mine; I paid for it. The money in your pocket came from my account. Leave everything that is mine in this house . . . and I want you to get out. You may keep the clothes on your back and the shoes on your feet . . . but that's it. There's the door. Leave now. When you decide to change your attitude and come back into this home as a family member with a cooperative, submissive spirit, we will accept you and welcome you back, but not until then! I love you and I always will, but you're not the boy we raised, and I'm not putting up with it one minute longer."

The boy stood to his feet, put all his money on the desk, walked to the door and left everything without saying one word. He proudly walked to the sidewalk out front, took a left, and got about three blocks down the street.

The boy stood there motionless with his hands in his empty pockets, thinking about all he would be facing, the street life he knew nothing about, and everything he was leaving behind . . . all the things back home he needed and longed for. He remembered his father's strong rebuke and also his promise to accept him back with an attitude of repentance.

When it was almost dark, he turned around, walked home with his head down, and knocked on his own front door. And then he confessed, "I'm wrong. I'm sorry. I realize I need you and I want all of you to know that I'm sorry. I love you." His entire family reached out and embraced him. The son's repentance changed everything.

How does this modern story of repentance impact you? What lifelong lesson do you think the son learned from his experience?

In Hosea 6:6, God says, "I delight in loyalty rather than sacrifice, and in the knowledge of God rather than burnt offerings." Jesus alluded to this verse in Matthew 9:13 when He told the Pharisees, "Go and learn what this means: 'I desire compassion, and not sacrifice.'" Our Father prefers a humble heart of worship over empty words and useless sacrifices.

Spend some time in prayer now, confessing your sin and offering God your loyalty and love. Ask Him for the strength to meet your current trials with courage, faith, and endurance. Finish with a prayer of thanksgiving for all of the blessings in your life.

19 *Finally, God's Justice Rolls Down*

Job 42:1–10

> My wrath is kindled against you and against your two friends, because you have not spoken of Me what is right as My servant Job has.
>
> —Job 42:7

In the autumn of 2002, the news media buzzed with the shocking accounts of a mysterious sniper on a killing spree, terrorizing people in the Washington, D.C., area. For over three weeks, this sniper brutally murdered innocent people by firing on them from the trunk of his car. He killed ten people and severely wounded four others, choosing his victims randomly over a 115-mile swath of real estate. Waves of fear and anxiety spread nationwide.

As Americans watched these vicious killings unfold on the news, we longed for the random and senseless murders to end. We prayed that the perpetrator would be found quickly and punished for his horrendous crimes.

Thankfully, the sniper's reign of terror ended on October 24, 2002, with an arrest at a Maryland rest stop. The sniper actually turned out to be a duo of cold-blooded killers: John Allen Muhammad and Lee Boyd Malvo. Americans breathed a collective sigh of relief as the killers were taken into custody, tried, and found guilty of murder. Finally, justice was served.

Sometimes we see justice done on earth, but many times, we don't. God, however, *always* acts justly. No one is better at administering justice than the Almighty, who is all-knowing and absolutely righteous. When His justice finally arrives, it's always worth the wait. That wait can seem interminably long, but it will come. Not all of God's accounts are settled at the end of each month, but *they will be settled*. Justice is a part of His character. He will not ignore sin . . . He cannot.

TREASURES FROM THE TEXT

God's Desires

Sometimes, justice occurs quickly. But other times, injustice seems to linger on forever! We lament the cruelty, hurt, and unfairness we see in the world. The Bible indicates that God the Father also is passionately concerned over the lack of justice He sees among His people. The prophet Amos records Yahweh's words as He expresses His desire for justice in Israel:

> I hate, I reject your festivals,
> Nor do I delight in your solemn assemblies.
> Even though you offer up to Me burnt offerings and your grain offerings,
> I will not accept them;
> And I will not even look at the peace offerings of your fatlings.
> Take away from Me the noise of your songs;
> I will not even listen to the sound of your harps.
> But let justice roll down like waters
> And righteousness like an ever-flowing stream. (Amos 5:21–24)

The Lord had gotten sick and tired of the people's hollow religious meetings, their busy conferences, their empty-hearted offerings, even their songs. He wasn't about to put up with the sham much longer; His fuse was now frighteningly short.

In *The Message,* Eugene Peterson renders the passage this way:

> I can't stand your religious meetings.
>   I'm fed up with your conferences and conventions.
> I want nothing to do with your religion projects,
>   your pretentious slogans and goals.
> I'm sick of your fund-raising schemes,
>   your public relations and image making.
> I've had all I can take of your noisy ego-music.
>   When was the last time you sang to *me?*

Do you know what I want?
I want justice—oceans of it.
I want fairness—rivers of it.
That's what I want. That's *all* I want. (Amos 5:21–24 MSG)

From this passage, what do you learn about God's desires?

What surprises you about God's words here?

We often struggle to understand God's timeline when it comes to righting the wrongs that have been done to His people. One man wrote, "The mills of God grind slowly, yet they grind exceedingly small."[1] God designed us to want justice, equity, and fairness, and we, like Job, don't like having to wait for justice to be served. We want the account to be settled *now*, not next month . . . or next year . . . or in eternity.

Our hearts soar and our souls feel satisfied when we see justice done, especially in the life of a person who has suffered undeservedly. Job was finally about to get the treatment and restoration he deserved, and his three friends were in for quite a surprise.

Job's Confession

Let's take a few moments to go back to Job's confession in 42:1–6. From this magnificent statement of faith, we can glean four important principles to apply to our lives.

1. *God's purpose is unfolding.* Job recognized that he could not hinder or thwart the plans and objectives of God.

Then Job answered the LORD and said,
"I know that You can do all things,
And that no purpose of Yours can be thwarted." (Job 42:1–2)

Often, when we're faced with seemingly insurmountable obstacles, we begin to wonder if God really does have a purpose for our lives. Events seem to happen in a random manner that defies explanation. Severe needs arise that leave us asking "Why, God? Don't You care?" As our lives seem to veer out of control, we wonder if God is present or powerful enough to change our circumstances. But as we trace the thread of Job's confession, we'll see that God had a plan all along.

2. *God's plan is incredible.* Job declares,

> "Who is this that hides counsel without knowledge?"
> Therefore I have declared that which I did not understand,
> Things too wonderful for me, which I did not know. (Job 42:3)

In this verse, Job repeated God's question to him and then made this assertion: He could not comprehend it. Job accepted the fact that God's ways are greater than our ways. God's thoughts don't always fit into our little boxes of human logic. His plan is deeper. His purposes are far more profound. We can't hinder them, nor can we comprehend them. But when we trust the heart of God and accept the fact that He cares for us, we can have peace even in the midst of suffering.

3. *God's instruction is reliable.* Job repeated in awe God's words to him and continued with his confession:

> "Hear, now, and I will speak;
> I will ask You, and You instruct me."
> I have heard of You by the hearing of the ear;
> But now my eye sees You. (Job 42:4–5)

Job didn't dare ignore God! He had heard the teaching and the mumblings of his friends, and he had heard the words of God. But nothing startled and awed Job as much as seeing God's hand and recognizing His sovereignty over the situation.

4. *God's way is best.* Seeing God's hand led Job to make his crowning statement of humility before God:

> Therefore I retract,
> And I repent in dust and ashes. (Job 42:6)

Job finally recanted and regretted his strong words against the Almighty. He realized that he couldn't resist the will of God. He understood that life was not all about Job, his suffering, and his desires; it was about God.

Taking Truth to Heart

We, too, need to be reminded that life is all about God. It's not about us. It's not about our comfort, our space, our rights, our will, our career, our salary, our plans, our home, our families, or our health. It's not about keeping up with the Joneses. Instead, it's about God's glory, His majesty, His power, and His desires for us. It's about His way, His will, and how He wants to use us to achieve His purposes in the world. Making God the center of our lives doesn't mean that our trials and difficulties will immediately exit stage left. But it does mean that we can have true joy no matter our circumstances.

In his confession, Job showed that he finally got it. He finally realized that God's plan is profound, that His reasoning is right, and that His ways are higher than he could ever understand. With that, Job waved the white flag of surrender and said in complete sincerity, "I retract, and I repent. I said things I shouldn't have said; I talked about things I knew nothing about; I became self-righteous in my own defense. Lord, please know that my heart is Yours. I humble myself before You. I place myself at Your disposal. Your purpose is right; Your plan is incredible; Your reproofs are reliable; Your way is best."

And that did it! When the Lord heard these humble words and felt the deep emotions of contrition welling up in Job's heart, when He witnessed the humility of his broken spirit and the teachability of Job's soul, mercy kicked in, and justice rolled down. We see poetic justice done as the Lord decided to use Job in the process of making his friends answer for their false, hurtful words and accusations.

Once you adjust your life to His ways, you'll be amazed at how the Lord will use you in others' lives. You will be many things for them: a reproof, a refuge, a point of hope, a reason to go on, a source of strength, a calming influence, and so much more. God may choose to use you as a vehicle to help restore those who've strayed far. And this often includes those who have hurt *you* in their straying.

God's Mercy

Once God perceived Job's repentant heart and heard his humble words of contrition, His mercy kicked in and His bountiful grace flowed down. In fact, God even used Job to help restore the three misguided friends to a right relationship with Him.

> It came about after the LORD had spoken these words to Job, that the LORD said to Eliphaz the Temanite, "My wrath is kindled against you and against your two friends, because you have not spoken of Me what is right as My servant Job has." (Job 42:7)

God felt deep displeasure with Job's three friends, and wasn't afraid to say so. He told them, "You've made Me angry. Your words have been misguided and false. Your actions have been wrong. My wrath is kindled against you."

Notice that God's anger burned only toward these three friends and not against the fourth friend, Elihu. Why is Elihu omitted? Probably because he, the last of the friends, was more right than wrong. He had been more on-target than the first three had been, though his perspective needed some minor adjustments and his pride needed to come down a few notches. Not being as guilty as Eliphaz, Bildad, and Zophar, he fell into a different category. Perhaps the Lord dealt with him later, choosing not to include that confrontation in Scripture.

We tend to be uncomfortable when God expresses His anger openly. Many of us have been taught that it's "ungodly" to be angry, and that Christians are never supposed to express their anger. Parents, teachers, pastors, and other leaders may have suggested that all anger is a sin, and we're wrong to express it. We may have been encouraged to "stuff" our uncomfortable feelings instead of releasing them by talking them out in a healthy way.

According to Scripture, however, there is a proper time and place for the expression of our anger. Almighty God expressed righteous indignation at certain times, and Jesus twice overturned the moneychangers' tables and chased them out of the temple with a whip (see Matthew 21:12; John 2:15).

We're never commanded in Scripture to refrain from expressing our anger if it is justified; however, we are commanded to deal with the problem rather than remaining angry and carrying a grudge. Paul wrote in Ephesians:

Therefore, laying aside falsehood, speak truth each one of you with his neighbor, for we are members of one another. Be angry, and yet do not sin; do not let the sun go down on your anger, and do not give the devil an opportunity. (Ephesians 4:25–27)

As you were growing up, how did your family handle anger? Do you feel it was managed positively or negatively?

How were you taught to deal with your own anger? Have your skills in dealing with anger improved as you have matured? If not, what needs to change?

Thankfully, it's not only God's justice that rolled down in the story of Job and his friends; God's mercy flowed freely, too. The Lord provided a means for Job's friends to confess their sin and be reconciled to Job and to Him for the wrongs they had committed.

Now therefore, take for yourselves seven bulls and seven rams, and go to My servant Job, and offer up a burnt offering for yourselves, and My servant Job will pray for you. For I will accept him so that I may not do with you according to your folly, because you have not spoken of Me what is right, as My servant Job has. (Job 42:8)

This passage reminds us of Jesus's teaching in the Sermon on the Mount:

Therefore if you are presenting your offering at the altar, and there remember that your brother has something against you, leave your offering there before the altar and go; first be reconciled to your brother, and then come and present your offering. (Matthew 5:23–24)

God doesn't want our gifts unless our hearts are right with Him and with others. But sometimes we try to appease Him by giving Him offerings or making deals with Him. We attempt to gloss over the wrongs we've done instead of humbly confessing them. But God's forgiveness doesn't work that way. He doesn't want our empty words and meaningless offerings; He wants our hearts.

Job, the offended one, then prayed for his offenders. In Job 42:8, God said, "For I will accept him." The Hebrew literally reads, "For I will lift his face up." In other words, "*I will accept his intercession on your behalf. As you lift up the offerings and Job prays for you, I will forgive your sins and treat you with mercy and compassion.*" For Job's sake, God would offer grace to Eliphaz, Bildad, and Zophar instead of the punishment they deserved!

Finally, Job's friends got their fill of humble pie as they were forced to admit the error of their ways and the prideful attitudes behind their sinful words. They brought their costly offerings (seven bulls) to the Lord, and Job prayed for them. As a result, God accepted their offering and restored them.

> So Eliphaz the Temanite and Bildad the Shuhite and Zophar the Naamathite went and did as the LORD told them; and the LORD accepted Job. (Job 42:9)

What a picture of God's grace! And what a picture of the justice and mercy that God poured forth at the cross of Christ! Just as the lifeblood flowed out of the bulls that Eliphaz, Bildad, and Zophar sacrificed as satisfaction for their sins, so also Jesus' blood was poured out on the cross for our sins. And just as God the Father accepted Job's intercession on his friends' behalf, so also He accepts Christ's intercession on our behalf. The apostle Paul wrote:

> Have this attitude in yourselves which was also in Christ Jesus, who, although He existed in the form of God, did not regard equality with God a thing to be grasped, but *emptied Himself,* taking the form of a bond-servant, and being made in the likeness of men. Being found in appearance as a man, He humbled Himself by becoming obedient to the point of death, even death on a cross. (Philippians 2:5–8, emphasis added)

In what ways did Christ "empty Himself" when he came to earth?

How can you "empty yourself" to serve those around you?

God allowed His Son to be humbled for a reason. Our heavenly Father loved us so much that He wanted to redeem us from the sin and death that we have chosen. But only a perfect, sinless sacrifice would satisfy His perfect justice, so He sent Jesus to become that sacrifice. Through Christ's life and death, God's purposes of redemption were fulfilled. Our role is to accept that gift of redemption and believe that Christ paid the price for our sins.

Eventually, in His time, not ours, God's justice will roll down as every person who has ever lived will recognize their sin, bow before the Son of God, and confess Jesus as Lord. Paul painted a vivid picture of this in Philippians 2:9–11:

> For this reason also, God highly exalted Him, and bestowed on Him the name which is above every name, so that at the name of Jesus every knee will bow, of those who are in heaven and on earth and under the earth, and that every tongue will confess that Jesus Christ is Lord, to the glory of God the Father.

Will we bow before Christ and live for Him now? Or will we wait until we stand before His throne in our utter sinfulness and realize that it's too late for us to choose to follow Him? Job chose to follow and obey God while he had the opportunity. And God never left him or forsook him, though it may have seemed so at the time. In fact, for Job's faithfulness throughout his painful ordeal, God poured out blessings upon him:

> The LORD restored the fortunes of Job when he prayed for his friends, and the LORD increased all that Job had twofold. (Job 42:10)

Because of Job's faith and his obedient, sacrificial prayer on behalf of those who had wronged him, God restored Job's fortunes and gave him back twice what he had lost. More important, Job realized that even when God seemed silent and distant, He had never left Job's side.

Why do you think it is important that Job's fortunes were restored?

How does it make you feel to know that Job was finally vindicated?

NUGGETS OF WISDOM

From the examples of Job's intercession for his friends and Christ's sacrifice for us, we can draw two truths for our lives. First, *forgiveness is worth asking for.* If you've spoken harsh words or harbored bitterness in your heart toward God or others, what's keeping you from confessing it? Bring that burden to the Lord. God delights in our humble confession. He promises to listen if you approach Him with a broken heart and a contrite spirit.

Have you approached anyone to ask for forgiveness as a result of what you've learned in this study? If not, is there still anyone whose forgiveness you need to seek?

Second, *justice is worth waiting for.* If justice comes immediately, thank the Lord for His provision. If it doesn't come immediately, wait for it. Enter into prayer about the situation and seek to discover the truths that God may be trying to teach you. He'll help you cultivate patience in the process.

Is there a current situation in your life in which you desire justice? If so, what is it?

How has your study of Job influenced your attitude toward this situation?

Often, we find that our longing for justice is based on our wanting God to deal with someone else's sin. We want Him to take our side and punish the person who is in the wrong. We want Him to honor and recognize our rights above the rights of others. But when we focus on serving God and others, forgiving people, loving them, and putting their rights above our own, we often find that our longing for vindication diminishes. We recognize that God's justice, tempered with His mercy and grace, is what we really need. And we should be willing to offer forgiveness to others as much as we need to receive it from our Father.

And Job Lived Happily Ever After . . . or Did He?

20

Job 42:10–17

> The LORD restored the fortunes of Job when he prayed for his friends, and the LORD increased all that Job had twofold.
>
> —Job 42:10

O NCE UPON A TIME . . .

When we hear these four words, we know that we're about to enter a fairy-tale land in which anything is possible. A poor little servant girl becomes the belle of the ball and catches the eye of a ravishing young prince. A sword-slinging knight defeats a fierce, fire-breathing dragon. A precocious young boy discovers that he never has to grow up. A gallant prince rescues a long-haired damsel from her castle-tower prison. A sleeping beauty awakens to her true love's kiss.

At the end of each imaginative tale, we know that we'll hear these six words: "and they lived happily ever after." We sigh with satisfaction, knowing that the kings and queens, princes and princesses, knights and dragons, evil stepmothers and wicked witches all got what they deserved—good or bad.

Unfortunately, real life's not a fairy tale. Maybe you're single, wondering if your "knight in shining armor" or "lady in waiting" will ever show up. If you are married, when you found "the one," that special person you wanted to spend your life with, you may have thought, "At last! This person will make me complete." But you soon discovered that your mate is as imperfect as you are.

Perhaps you finally had a chance to build your "dream house," and then you found that it was anything but. Or maybe you got a new job and thought, "Finally! This is going to bring me the career status and fulfillment I've been longing for." But that didn't happen. Or maybe when you had your first baby, your expectations were off the chart . . . until you realized that the little darling is not always as darling as you first believed.

Our responses to life's circumstances indicate that we're still longing for the fairy tale. When we come to the end of a great story, whether it's in a movie, a novel, or the Bible, we want the hero or heroine to live happily ever after—especially when that person has suffered as much as Job.

When you were a child, what was your favorite fairy tale? What made it so significant to you?

In a very real sense, Job's life did have a fairy-tale ending, as we shall see. The question is, why? What paved the way for a happy ending for Job? Let's read on to find out.

Treasures from the Text

Before we continue our journey through Job 42, let's look back at an earlier verse in the story—Job 23:10. This verse, part of Job's reply to Eliphaz, illustrates that Job had faith in God's sovereignty and that he trusted the Lord to vindicate him of all false accusations. The verse reads, "But He knows the way I take; When He has tried me, I shall come forth as gold."

Three items are noteworthy in this verse. First, Job believed that God knew his situation. Second, Job believed that God was testing him. And third, Job believed that, after the trials ended, he would emerge a better man. Though he didn't know the details of his eventual restoration, he anticipated answers from God.

Fast forward now to Job 42:10. This verse appears in the book's prose epilogue, which describes how God restored Job's reputation, family, and fortunes. Mike Mason writes,

> After thirty-nine chapters of passionate poetry, the return to prose in the Epilogue comes as something of a relief. One cannot live continually on the level of intensity represented by poetry. Returning to ordinary life after a mountaintop experience of God is largely what faith is all about.[1]

The poetry of Job has taken us from the mountaintops of blessing to the deepest valleys of despair and back again. But thankfully, instead of having to listen to more of Job's anguished laments and his friends' self-righteous speeches, we've reached the happy ending of Job's tale. For his blamelessness, tenacity, and faith, Job receives four specific blessings from God.

One: *God doubled Job's possessions.*

> The LORD restored the fortunes of Job when he prayed for his friends, and the LORD increased all that Job had twofold. (Job 42:10)

Although God didn't owe Job anything, He graciously made restitution for all that Job had lost. Yahweh received the prayers and offerings of Job for his friends, and He poured out a double measure of blessings upon His servant.

Two: *God restored Job's relatives and friends.*

> Then all his brothers and all his sisters and all who had known him before came to him, and they ate bread with him in his house; and they consoled him and comforted him for all the adversities that the LORD had brought on him. And each one gave him one piece of money, and each a ring of gold. The LORD blessed the latter days of Job more than his beginning; and he had 14,000 sheep and 6,000 camels and 1,000 yoke of oxen and 1,000 female donkeys. (Job 42:11–12)

During his painful times of suffering, Job had felt excruciating isolation and a depth of loneliness that few of us can imagine. But now, God sent Job's brothers, sisters, relatives, and friends to console and comfort him. Not only did they offer words of encouragement and restoration, but they also provide Job with tangible support by giving him money and gold rings. In addition, God multiplied Job's flocks and herds so that they would be a source of wealth for him.

Clearly, Job was blessed with more than enough possessions and riches. How do you tend to feel around people who have many more possessions than you do?

What lessons have you learned from Job's experience that can help you guard yourself against envy and covetousness?

Three: *God blessed Job and his wife with ten more children.*

> He had seven sons and three daughters. He named the first Jemimah, and the second Keziah, and the third Keren-happuch. In all the land no women were found so fair as Job's daughters; and their father gave them inheritance among their brothers. (Job 42:13–15)

Surprisingly, the names of Job's three daughters are listed, while those of his seven sons are omitted. John E. Hartley writes, "The daughters' names are *Jemimah,* 'turtle-dove,' a name used for graceful birds, plants, or precious stones; *Keziah,* the name of the aromatic plant *cassia,* a prized variety of cinnamon; and *Keren-Happuch,* a horn of eye paint, i.e., black rouge used to highlight the eyes."[2]

Windows to the Ancient World

Job's preferential treatment of these three beautiful girls surely turned many heads in his culture. Mike Mason writes this about Job's relationship with his daughters:

With all that might have been said about the glory of Job's latter days, why was this information about his daughters singled out for special mention? The very oddity of the passage may be a clue to its importance, for at the time it was written (and for long afterwards) it must have struck its readers as being not just odd but outrageous. That the names of Job's daughters should be specifically mentioned while those of the sons are omitted, and furthermore that the daughters should be given equal inheritance with the sons—this was not conventional Old Testament protocol. Indeed to most of the societies of the ancient world such treatment of women would have seemed not merely eccentric, but politically subversive. To give women a landed inheritance is to give them equal status; it is to take them out of the kitchen and make them managers, owners, merchants, voters, and finally lawmakers and rulers. How far ahead of his time Job was![3]

Job's sons received a vast inheritance, yet his daughters also received special treatment and part of the inheritance as well. What does this tell us about the place of his children in Job's heart?

Older parents often come to parenthood with a different perspective and attitude than younger parents. In what ways do you think Job's relationship with these ten children was different than his relationship with the first ten? Why?

Four: *God blessed Job with a long, satisfying life.*

> After this, Job lived 140 years, and saw his sons and his grandsons, four generations. And Job died, an old man and full of days. (Job 42:16–17)

Since God doubled everything for Job, Job must have been seventy years old when this story began. God allowed him to live twice as many years (140) in addition to those seventy. He died at a ripe old age after living a rich, full life with his wife, sons, and daughters. Warren Wiersbe writes: "To die 'old and full of years' was the goal of every person. It means more than a long life; it means a rich and full life that ends well."[4]

Another author expands on this description of Job's fullness of life:

> When Job died he was "full of years," a Biblical expression signifying not merely longevity but fullness of wisdom and godliness. To be full of years is to have seen everything there is to see and to have done everything there is to do, to the point that now one is so full of it all that there is no room for anything else. There is no room for any more time or any more world; one is crammed to the gills with it.[5]

What experiences and adventures would you like to have had when you come to the end of your life?

What character qualities would you like to have developed by then?

Why do you think Job was able to die "full of years"? Was it because of the blessings he had received from God? Was it because of the way he had lived his life? Was it both? Explain your answer.

Do you know any older people who have many outward blessings but are unable to truly enjoy them because of the way they have lived life? Do you know any who are able to enjoy blessings because of how they have lived? What is the difference you see in the two types of people?

If you could write your own epitaph, what would you want it to say?

NUGGETS OF WISDOM

Job modeled a vibrant, God-honoring, fulfilled life. How can we do the same? Consider these five tips for staying young at heart and living life well.

Keep developing your mind. Take every opportunity to learn something new. Seek to know God and others better. Travel. Read a good book. Pick up a new hobby. Learn to play an instrument. Go back to school to study what you've always wanted to study. No matter your age, you can keep your mind sharp by taking on new challenges.

Keep enjoying your humor. Dale Evans Rogers wrote this humorous prayer that deals with the realities of life:

Lord, thou knowest better than I know myself, that I am growing older, and will someday be old.

Keep me from getting talkative, and particularly from the fatal habit of thinking I must say something on every subject and on every occasion.

Release me from the craving to try and straighten out everybody's affairs.

Keep my mind free from the recital of endless details—give me wings to get to the point.

I ask for grace enough to listen to the tales of others' pains. Help me endure them with patience.

But seal my lips on my own aches and pains. They are increasing, and my love of rehearsing them is becoming sweeter as the years go by. . . .

Teach me the glorious lesson that occasionally I may be mistaken. . . .

Make me thoughtful, but not moody; helpful, but not bossy.

With my vast store of wisdom, it seems a pity not to use it; but Thou knowest, Lord, I want a few friends at the end.

Give me the ability to see good things in unexpected places, and talents in unexpected people. And give me, Lord, the grace to tell them so.[6]

What steps can you take to be a little less serious and see the humor in your life's circumstances?

What hobbies and activities do you enjoy that help you to relax?

Keep using your strength. In spiritual matters, as well as physical, this motto is true: Use it or lose it! Continue to exercise your mental, spiritual, and physical muscles in order to remain strong and healthy. Use your gifts to serve others in your home, workplace, church, and community.

In what ways can you use your talents and strengths to serve those around you?

If you aren't currently involved in your church, in which area would you most like to serve? Contact someone this week to find out more about this ministry opportunity.

Keep pursuing your opportunities. Maybe you've always dreamed of taking a mission trip to China. Or scaling Mount Everest. Or leading a Bible study at your church. Or learning to play the piano. Or teaching youth. Or quitting your job to stay home with your children. Or changing careers so you can pursue God's call on your life. Whatever open doors and golden opportunities God brings your way, seize them! Why put off until tomorrow something you can do today?

What are your top three goals for the next year?

How do you plan to achieve these goals?

Keep seeking and serving God. Make the Lord your first priority. Make your pursuit of Him your number one passion, and you'll sense His restoration, His blessing, and His protection on your life.

What other pursuits seem to infringe upon your personal time with God?

How can you make your quiet time and personal devotions more meaningful?

Taking Truth to Heart

Isn't it good to know that God understands that our best-laid plans often fail? He knows all about our desires, our failures and successes, our deepest despair and our most secret sorrows. When you feel discouraged and need some direction for Bible reading and prayer, turn to the Psalms—the poignant prayer-songs of struggling believers. They hold meaningful, relevant promises for those of us who suffer.

In Psalm 37:3–4, David wrote:

> Trust in the LORD and do good;
> Dwell in the land and cultivate faithfulness.
> Delight yourself in the LORD;
> And He will give you the desires of your heart.

Psalm 126:5–6 says:

> Those who sow in tears shall reap with joyful shouting.
> He who goes to and fro weeping, carrying his bag of seed,
> Shall indeed come again with a shout of joy, bringing his sheaves with him.

And Psalm 30:4–5 reads:

> Sing praise to the LORD, you His godly ones,
> And give thanks to His holy name.
> For His anger is but for a moment,
> His favor is for a lifetime;
> Weeping may last for the night,
> But a shout of joy comes in the morning.

What promises from these verses can we cling to when trials come?

When we praise God and center our lives around Him, we can give thanks, no matter our circumstances. Though our weeping and sorrow may last for a night, our shout of joy will come in the morning. If we, like Job, cling to our faith, we can rest assured that there will be a happy ending to our fairy tale as well.

21 *What Job Teaches Us about Ourselves*

Selections from Job

> Remember that my life is but breath.
>
> —Job 7:7

Asign on a church bulletin board read, "Christ is the answer." Next to it, someone had written, "Yes, but what's the question?"[1]

Isn't this true of life? In order to have the answer, we naturally must first be aware of the question. And in order to ask the right question, we must be aware of a particular need. Sometimes God uses suffering to do just that—to make us aware of our need, to make us realize there are questions we need answered. Questions like, Who's in control? How should I respond to the unfairness I see in the world? Why doesn't my loved one's illness get better? What happens when we die?

Christians have the truth that others need to hear! But nonbelievers must be *aware* of their need before they'll be motivated to seek answers to life's most important questions. God can use suffering for good in their lives, too. In this sense, we can be thankful for suffering, because it can make *all of us* aware of our desperate need for God.

Through his suffering, Job recognized his utter dependence upon God. His faith enabled him to withstand his trials, yet his excruciatingly painful experiences left certain questions unanswered. When God met him in the midst of the storm, though, all that mattered was that the Almighty One was on the throne.

To gain perspective on the lessons God wants to teach us through this book, let's take a step back and look at the big picture. We'll take seven important principles from Job's experience and apply them to our own lives.

TREASURES FROM THE TEXT

Seven Principles for Today

1. *We never know ahead of time the plans God has for us.* To illustrate this, return to the beginning of Job for a moment. Remember the wonderful blessings that Job enjoyed when you were first introduced to him in Job 1?

> There was a man in the land of Uz whose name was Job; and that man was blameless, upright, fearing God and turning away from evil. Seven sons and three daughters were born to him. His possessions also were 7,000 sheep, 3,000 camels, 500 yoke of oxen, 500 female donkeys, and very many servants; and that man was the greatest of all the men of the east. (Job 1:1–3)

Job began as "the greatest of all the men of the east." No ordinary man, he possessed integrity, righteousness, respect, and riches—and yet he went through the most horrible experiences imaginable.

Job had no clue when the sun came up on that fateful day that his entire life would soon be turned completely upside down. He saw no early-morning skywriting. He received no angelic visit. He heard no tap at the window. He sensed no omen suggesting that all hell was about to break loose.

Instead, he simply got up and went about his daily business: checking on the livestock, examining the crops in the fields, chatting with his servants, taking a trip into town to do business, coming home in the evening to relax and have dinner with his wife. But then he received a round of heart-wrenching news from a messenger. Then a second. And a third. And a fourth. Before he could sneeze, his livestock had been seized, his servants slain, and his ten children killed by a freak windstorm. Everything he had worked for throughout his entire life suddenly lay smoldering in a heap of ashes.

Yet even on that darkest of days, Job clung to his faith in God's love and His divine sovereignty. Job's trust is evident in his remarkably humble response to his calamity.

> Then Job arose and tore his robe and shaved his head, and he fell to the ground and worshiped.

228

He said,

> "Naked I came from my mother's womb,
> And naked I shall return there.
> The LORD gave and the LORD has taken away.
> Blessed be the name of the LORD."
> Through all this Job did not sin nor did he blame God. (Job 1:20–22)

Amazing! Can you imagine yourself responding like that? It may seem impossible, but the good news is, if you're a believer, you are supernaturally empowered through the indwelling of the Holy Spirit to do just that. When we're blindsided by life's calamities, we can hold fast to the promises that we find in God's Word. We read in Jeremiah:

> "For I know the plans that I have for you," declares the LORD, "plans for welfare and not for calamity to give you a future and a hope. Then you will call upon Me and come and pray to Me, and I will listen to you. You will seek Me and find Me when you search for Me with all your heart." (Jeremiah 29:11–13)

Notice that God doesn't tell His people: "I know the plans that I have for you, and I'll tell you all about them ahead of time so you'll know what to expect." He simply says, "I know the future. Trust Me. Call upon Me. Pray to Me. Seek Me. Search for Me." Not only that, but He promises us that when we seek Him, we'll find Him. He promises to hear our prayers and to respond with grace, love, peace, and forgiveness.

2. *A vertical perspective will keep us from horizontal panic.* You may have noticed something about Job's responses: He never once blamed God (or Satan, for that matter) for his suffering. In fact, he had no awareness of the dialogue that had occurred between God and Satan in the heavenly realm. Yet Job kept a vertical perspective. He knew that God had allowed this calamity to befall him, but he also knew that God provided his only hope for restoration.

What circumstances or distractions sometimes hinder you from having a vertical focus?

How can you minimize or eliminate these distractions in your life, either by changing your circumstances or by changing your focus in the midst of them?

3. *Great discernment is needed to detect wrong advice from a well-meaning person.* Remember the not-so-wise advice that Job's wife gave him? "Do you still hold fast your integrity? Curse God and die!" (Job 2:9).

Job's wife meant to help end his suffering, but her advice was flawed. She actually encouraged Job to do what Satan wanted him to do: "curse God and die." But Job refused to compromise his faith: "You speak as one of the foolish women speaks. Shall we indeed accept good from God and not accept adversity? In all this Job did not sin with his lips" (Job 2:10).

When have you received wrong advice from a well-meaning person? How did you handle the situation?

How can you gain spiritual discernment and insight into a person's situation before sharing your words of wisdom?

4. *When things turn from bad to worse, sound theology helps us remain strong and stable.* Cartoonist Charles Schultz addressed this principle in his Peanuts comic strip. One cartoon features Lucy and Linus looking out a picture window at a steady downpour of rain.

> "Boy, look at it rain!" exclaims Lucy. "What if it floods the whole world?"
> "It will never do that," Linus replies confidently. "In the ninth chapter of Genesis,

God promised Noah that would never happen again, and the sign of that promise is the rainbow."

"You've taken a great load off my mind," says Lucy.

"Sound theology has a way of doing that," Linus responds matter-of-factly.[2]

Sound theology does have a way of easing our minds in tough times. Just as emergency drills help us prepare for a disaster, knowing God's Word and having a strong relationship with Him provide us a shelter from life's storms. The knowledge and wisdom that we glean from Scripture enables us to stand on God's truth when suffering comes.

5. *Sensitive and caring friends know when to show up, when to stay quiet, and what to say when the time is right.* When Job's friends first heard of the tragedy that had struck, they left the comfort of their homes to come and stay by Job's side. Scripture paints a descriptive picture of their visit:

> Now when Job's three friends heard of all this adversity that had come upon him . . . they made an appointment together to come to sympathize with him and comfort him. When they lifted up their eyes at a distance and did not recognize him, they raised their voices and wept. And each of them tore his robe and they threw dust over their heads toward the sky. Then they sat down on the ground with him for seven days and seven nights with no one speaking a word to him, for they saw that his pain was very great. (Job 2:11–13)

The three men sympathized with Job and shared in the depth of his grief. They comforted Job with their presence and support without saying a word . . . until chapter 8, when Bildad began to unleash the flow of accusations.

Those of us who have been hospitalized or have been through a crisis know how reassuring the presence of a friend or family member can be. Even a small gesture like a simple touch, a pat on the back, a sympathetic squeeze of a hand, or a whispered prayer can make an enormous difference in the life of a suffering person.

How can you demonstrate sensitivity to the needs of those in your life who may be struggling?

6. *It's easy to be "armchair quarterbacks" when we encounter and respond to another's suffering.* When we read Job 3, we can sense that Job had reached the bottom of the pit of his despair. He cursed the day of his birth, wishing that he had never seen daylight. But instead of commiserating with Job, his friends judged him for uttering such strong words.

In Other Words

Author and pastor Eugene Peterson offers this advice for consoling a suffering friend:

When we rush in to fix suffering, we need to keep in mind several things. First, no matter how insightful we may be, we don't *really* understand the full nature of our friends' problems. Second, our friends may not *want* our advice. Third, the ironic fact of the matter is that more often than not, people do not suffer *less* when they are committed to following God, but *more.* When these people go through suffering, their lives are often transformed, deepened, marked with beauty and holiness, in remarkable ways that could never have been anticipated before the suffering.

So, instead of continuing to focus on preventing suffering—which we simply won't be very successful at anyway—perhaps we should begin *entering* the suffering, participating insofar as we are able—entering the mystery and looking around for God. In other words, we need to quit feeling sorry for people who suffer and instead look up to them, learn from them, and—if they will let us—join them in protest and prayer. Pity can be nearsighted and condescending; shared suffering can be dignifying and life-changing. As we look at Job's suffering and praying and worshiping, we see that he has already blazed a trail of courage and integrity for us to follow.[3]

Do you tend to rush in to try to fix suffering in people's lives? Why or why not?

What is your most difficult struggle at this point in your life? What makes it so difficult?

How can you "enter" your suffering in order to learn the most from it and be transformed into the image of Christ through it?

7. *The cultivation of obedient endurance is a mark of maturity.* As we continue to obey God, even though we don't know all the answers, we gain maturity as an outworking of our faith. Author Henry T. Blackaby writes:

> *Faith* is developed in real-life situations. "Sight" is not "faith." We constantly want God to "show us Your will for my life" even after He has assured us that He is doing just that. But God will do it in His way and in His time. . . . He does not need *our* help; we need *His* help! The "silences" of God do not mean He is late, or inactive, or not working. It means that this is where *faith* works![4]

The author of the book of Hebrews described the essential nature of faith this way: "And without faith it is impossible to please Him, for he who comes to God must believe that He is and that He is a rewarder of those who seek Him" (Hebrews 11:6).

In what ways has God used past faith tests, trials, and periods of suffering to build your faith?

Think of a difficult situation in which you made the decision to obey God, no matter the cost. How did the Lord use this experience to cultivate maturity in your life?

Taking Truth to Heart

If you had to choose one word to describe Job, what would it be? Most of us would probably think of patient, enduring, faithful, or something of that nature. But what about *passionate?* The story of Job reflects this man's passion to live for God, his passion for justice and truth, his passion to live a righteous life no matter the cost, and his passion to maintain his integrity in the face of false allegations.

How can we exhibit the same passion for God? How can we intensify our enthusiasm for life? How can we move from a day-by-day toleration of the status quo to a renewal of our desire to really come alive and worship Him with all our heart, soul, and mind?

The conductor of the Boston Philharmonic Orchestra, Benjamin Zander, gives us some insight into passionate living with two illustrations:

A young pianist was playing a Chopin prelude in my master class, and although we had worked right up to the edge of realizing an overarching concept of the piece, his performance remained earthbound. He understood it intellectually, he could have explained it to someone else, but he was unable to convey the emotional energy that is the true language of music. Then I noticed something that proved to be the key:

His body was firmly centered in the upright position. I blurted out, "The trouble is you're a two-buttock player!" I encouraged him to allow his whole body to flow sideways, urging him to catch the wave of the music with the shape of his own body, and suddenly the music took flight. Several in the audience gasped, feeling the emotional dart hit home, as a new distinction was born: the *one-buttock* player. The president of a corporation in Ohio, who was present as a witness, wrote to me: "I was so moved that I went home and transformed my whole company into a *one-buttock* company."

I never did find out what he meant by that, but I have my own ideas.

I met Jacqueline DuPre in the 1950s, when I was twenty and she was fifteen, a gawky English schoolgirl who blossomed into the greatest cellist of her generation. We performed the Two Cello Quintet of Schubert together, and I remember her playing was like a tidal wave of intensity and passion. When she was six years old, the story goes, she went into her first competition as a cellist, and she was seen running down the corridor carrying her cello above her head, with a huge grin of excitement on her face. A custodian, noting what he took to be relief on the little girl's face, said, "I see you've just had your chance to play!" And Jackie answered, excitedly, "No, no, I'm just about to!"

Even at six, Jackie was a conduit for music to pour through. She had the kind of radical confidence about her own highly personal expression that people acquire when they understand that performance is not about getting your act together, but about opening up to the energy of the audience and of the music, and letting it sing in your unique voice.[5]

Our goal is to become passionate players, not satisfied with pounding out another year of dull, predictable scales and chords, but throwing ourselves into our pursuit of God, playing the music of our lives with passion and vigor.

What people, things, and activities are you passionate about? How do you demonstrate your passion for them?

How passionate is your pursuit of God and His will right now? Is anyone or anything standing in the way of your ability to experience greater passion? If so, who or what is it?

NUGGETS OF WISDOM

Along with Job and other Old Testament saints, many New Testament believers maintained their passion for loving and serving God in the face of severe trials and faith tests. The apostle Peter wrote letters to suffering, persecuted believers scattered throughout Asia Minor. He warned them to be aware of Satan's destructive schemes and encouraged them to stand firmly rooted in the truth of God's Word. Peter exhorted his struggling brothers and sisters in the faith to love one another, to follow the example of Christ, to share Christ's sufferings, and to serve God willingly. He wrote:

> Therefore humble yourselves under the mighty hand of God, that He may exalt you at the proper time, casting all your anxiety on Him, because He cares for you. Be of sober spirit, be on the alert. Your adversary, the devil, prowls around like a roaring lion, seeking someone to devour. But resist him, firm in your faith, knowing that the same experiences of suffering are being accomplished by your brethren who are in the world. After you have suffered for a little while, the God of all grace, who called you to His eternal glory in Christ, will Himself perfect, confirm, strengthen and establish you. (1 Peter 5:6–10)

What reassuring promises can you glean from these verses?

Read Ephesians 6:10–17. How can you arm yourself to remain firmly rooted in your faith and to fend off Satan's evil schemes?

As we come full circle in the story of Job, we recognize that Phillip Yancey was right: The book really does center on *faith* more than it focuses on *suffering.* Job's trying time of suffering finally ended, but his legacy of faith has remained as a source of hope, comfort, and encouragement for every generation to follow. Hebrews 11:1–2 reads, "Now faith is the assurance of things hoped for, the conviction of things not seen. For by it the men of old gained approval."

When we faithfully, passionately seek after God, we find ourselves paying less attention to the temporal and the externals. We give increasingly more time to the eternal—to what is going on deep within. Soul searching replaces channel surfing. We start asking questions that are hard to answer. We think much more deeply about the things Job is teaching us. We focus on what matters—what would be left if all our material possessions and our lesser priorities were stripped away.

Friedrich Nietzsche referred to our lifelong faith journey as "a long obedience in the same direction."[6] When we follow the example of our forefathers and choose to follow in their footsteps of faith, we gain the Lord's approval . . . and greater spiritual maturity as well.

What Job Teaches Us about Our God

Selections from Job

> Then Job answered the LORD and said,
> "I know that You can do all things."
>
> —Job 42:1–2

IT'S AMAZING HOW MISCOMMUNICATION can lead to misunderstanding.

A couple from Minneapolis decided to escape Minnesota's frigid February temperatures by enjoying a long weekend together in Florida, relaxing on the beach. Due to their different work schedules, the husband decided to leave a day early, and his wife planned to meet him the next day in Florida.

When the husband got to the hotel, he pulled out his laptop and sent his wife an e-mail back in Minneapolis. However, he accidentally left one letter off her e-mail address, and the e-mail went to another person without his knowledge.

In Houston, a widow had just returned home from the funeral of her beloved husband, who had been a minister for many years and had been "called home to glory" following a sudden heart attack. The widow checked her e-mail, expecting condolence messages from relatives and friends. Upon reading the first message, however, she fainted and fell to the floor. The widow's son heard the noise and rushed into the room. He turned and saw this message on the computer screen:

To: My loving wife
From: Your departed husband
Subject: I've arrived!

Message: I've just arrived and have been checked in. Everything went very smoothly after my departure. I also verified that everything has been prepared for your arrival tomorrow. Looking forward to seeing you then! Hope your journey is as uneventful as mine was.

P.S. It sure is hot down here![1]

In the same way that this widow received a startling, confusing message, the stories we read in Scripture can at times be surprising and troubling. Why would a good God allow his chosen people, the Jews, to live in bondage for over four hundred years? How could a holy God call King David, an adulterer and murderer, "a man after My own heart"? And how could a compassionate, loving God allow a blameless man like Job to suffer so much?

Each of these questions has answers. They're not simple answers, and they won't satisfy everyone. But how these biblical characters lived teaches us lessons about our God. He's a God with a purpose and a plan. He wants us to become mature and faith-filled, but sometimes we must suffer in order to grow. And no one embodies this faith in the face of suffering better than our hero, Job.

Treasures from the Text

In the previous chapter, we learned seven lessons about ourselves from the experiences and responses of Job. In this chapter, we'll discover seven aspects of God's character that are illuminated by the light of Job's faith. Is God truly sovereign? Just? Faithful? Loving? Just ask Job.

1. *There is nothing God cannot do:*

> Then Job answered the LORD and said,
> "I know that You can do all things." (Job 42:1–2)

Here, Job refers to God's omnipotence, or limitless power. Job now knows that nothing and no one can limit, put conditions on, or in any way hinder the activities, acts, and works of our heavenly Father. God created us from nothing without losing one volt of His energy. He sustains all life without assistance. He even raises from the dead those He wishes to raise. Nothing stands in God's way. That's why only He deserves to be described as "awesome."

How have you experienced God's power in your life?

2. *It is impossible to restrain or nullify God's purposes.* Job recognized this truth when he stated, "No purpose of Yours can be thwarted" (Job 42:2). Author John E. Hartley writes:

> Yahweh's words have reaffirmed Job's conviction of his wise and judicious governance of the world. With an enhanced awareness of Yahweh's lordship, Job concedes that *no purpose (mezinna,* i.e., "detailed plans") of Yahweh's *can be foiled* or thwarted *(bāsar).* Job's concession means that he believes that everything occurring on earth takes place within the framework of the divine wisdom. No hostile force, be it earthly or heavenly, prevents God from carrying out his purpose.[2]

God's intentions can be neither altered nor disrupted. His purposes will transpire without delay, without hindrance, and without failure. Nothing surprises God. Nothing catches Him off guard. He knows the past hurts and sorrows that you carry with you. He also knows your present needs—emotional, physical, and spiritual. No matter how impossible your circumstances may seem, God's sovereignty and love are great enough to handle them all.

Currently, what are your greatest needs? List them here, and take a few minutes to talk to God about them right now.

3. *God's plans are beyond our understanding and too deep for us to explain.* In verse 3, Job admitted:

> Therefore I have declared that which I did not understand,
> Things too wonderful for me, which I did not know. (Job 42:3)

This confession required humility on Job's part. Some suggest that this verse represents the core message of the entire book: that the mystery of God's plan is too wonderful and too deep for us to fathom. But because we can't see ahead to the end of the story, we tend to wrestle with this mystery. And often we feel just plain disappointed with God. We recognize that He has a plan, but we don't know its full extent or its details. We don't know what part we're supposed to play in it. We don't know what to do next. We don't understand why certain things happen to some people and not others.

In Other Words

Phillip Yancey addresses this sense of disappointment best, writing,

I can think of several helpful things God could have said: "Job, I'm truly sorry about what's happened. You've endured many unfair trials on my behalf, and I'm proud of you. You don't know what this means to me and even to the universe." A few compliments, a dose of compassion, or at the least a brief explanation of what transpired "behind the curtain" in the unseen world—any of these would have given Job some solace.

God says nothing of the kind. His "reply," in fact, consists of more questions than answers. Sidestepping thirty-five chapters' worth of debates on the problem of pain, he plunges instead into a magnificent verbal tour of the natural world. . . .

In his book *Wishful Thinking,* Frederick Buechner sums up God's speech. "God doesn't explain. He explodes. He asks Job who he thinks he is anyway. He says that to try to explain the kind of things Job wants explained would be like trying to explain Einstein to a little-neck clam. . . . God doesn't reveal his grand design. He reveals himself." The message behind the splendid poetry boils down to this: *Until you know a little more about running the physical universe, Job, don't tell me how to run the moral universe.*

"Why are you treating me so unfairly, God?" Job has whined throughout the book. "Put yourself in my place."

"NO!!!" God thunders in reply. "You put yourself in *my* place! Until you can offer lessons on how to make the sun come up each day, or where to scatter lightning bolts, or how to design a hippopotamus, don't judge how I run the world. Just shut up and listen."

The impact of God's speech on Job is almost as amazing as the speech itself. Although God never answers question one about Job's predicament, the blast from the storm flattens Job. He repents in dust and ashes, and every trace of disappointment with God is swept away.[3]

We tend to channel our disappointment with life's circumstances into a misguided disappointment with God. What we don't realize is that God is the only One who will *never* disappoint us. People, situations, material things, our careers, our plans for the future—all these can and will disappoint us at one time or another. Only God can assure us that He'll always be the same (Hebrews 13:8). He'll always be there when we call, and He will always answer, though perhaps not according to our timeline or in the way we might think is best. Injustices happen as a result of sin in the world, not as a result of God's failure to keep His promises. He's faithful!

Have you ever felt disappointment with God? If so, when?

What do you think was the *true* basis for your disappointment?

4. *Only through God's instruction are we able to humble ourselves and rest in His will.* Once God arrived on the scene, Job humbly recognized that he had misspoken:

> I have heard of You by the hearing of the ear;
> But now my eye sees You;
> Therefore I retract,
> And I repent in dust and ashes. (Job 42:5–6)

Notice that God made no threat. He didn't force Job to get down on his knees. He just showed up, and Job immediately prostrated himself in humility and worship. In essence, Job pleaded, "Lord, instruct me. I will willingly submit to You. I will humbly accept the lessons that You have to teach me." Instead of clinging to his rights, Job released them. He didn't approach God with a sense of entitlement. He didn't bring expectations or demands. He didn't come to the Lord with arguments or a sullen demeanor.

You may be tempted to say, "Well, if God had blessed me like He blessed Job, I'd have the same response." But when Job spoke these words, he was still sitting on the ash heap in excruciating pain, covered with worm-infested boils. His children lay in graves. His wife had advised him to "curse God and die." His beautiful home, fields, livestock, and servants had been destroyed. He had lost everything, and he wasn't sure that God would ever restore his fortunes and family. Yet he still knelt in the dust in repentance before Yahweh.

What lessons can we learn from Job's godly, humble response?

5. *When the day of reckoning arrives, God is always fair.* You can rest assured that God is keeping tabs on every person who has ever lived. Not a single idle thought, word, or action slips His attention. According to His timetable, He blesses those who walk with Him and deals severely with wrongdoers. The author of Hebrews wrote: "For God is not unjust so as to forget your work and the love which you have shown toward His name, in having ministered and in still ministering to the saints" (Hebrews 6:10).

God doesn't forget our words or actions. He made it clear in Job 42:7 that He had heard every false and accusing word that Job's friends had spoken:

> It came about after the LORD had spoken these words to Job, that the LORD said to Eliphaz the Temanite, "My wrath is kindled against you and against your two friends, because you have not spoken of Me what is right as My servant Job has."

He heard! Though Yahweh may not have responded at the time, He had listened to one unfair accusation after another against Job. He didn't overlook a single wrong that had been done against His servant. His wrath was kindled against Job's friends, and He commanded them to present a burnt offering "so that I may not do with you according to your folly, because you have not spoken of Me what is right, as My servant Job has" (Job 42:8).

How do you respond to the fact that God knows your every thought, hears your every word, and sees your every action?

Read Romans 8:33–39. What assurances concerning God does this passage provide us as believers?

6. *No one can be compared to God when it comes to offering blessings.* Job 42:10–12 records the restoration of Job's possessions and family:

> The LORD restored the fortunes of Job when he prayed for his friends, and the Lord increased all that Job had twofold. Then all his brothers and all his sisters and all who had known him before came to him, and they ate bread with him in his house; and they consoled him and comforted him for all the adversities that the LORD had brought on him. And each one gave him one piece of money, and each a ring of gold. The LORD blessed the latter days of Job more than his beginning.

Notice the merciful works of God in these verses: The Lord *restored.* The Lord *increased.* The Lord *blessed.* He poured out words and acts of grace upon His suffering servant Job. In our culture, which seems to thrive on bad news and shocking exposés, we cling to stories like this one that so clearly demonstrate God's love, grace, restoration, and forgiveness.

What are the greatest blessings God has given you? How do you show your thankfulness for these blessings?

7. Only God can fill our final years with divine music that frees us to live above our circumstances.

Taking Truth to Heart

Author Ken Gire offers this soul-stirring example in his book *The Reflective Life:*

The movie [*The Shawshank Redemption*] is about prisoners in the Shawshank prison, struggling to hold onto their humanity. Andy, played by Tim Robbins, is there struggling too. He carves chessmen from stone, petitions the state for books for the prison library, and helps inmates get their high school diploma. These are a few of the ways he holds on to his humanity. One other way costs him two weeks in solitary confinement when he gains access to the prison's public address system and plays a record for the entire prison to hear.

As the music streams through the washroom and prison yard, the inmates stop and stand transfixed. The actor, Morgan Freeman, a friend of Andy's and narrator of the story, says these words about that moment: "I have no idea to this day what those two Italian ladies were singing about. Truth is, I don't wanna know. Some things are best left unsaid. I'd like to think they were singing about something so beautiful it can't be expressed in words and makes your heart ache because of it. I tell you those voices soared, higher and farther than anybody in the great place dared to dream. It was like some beautiful bird flapped into Alexander's cage and made those walls dissolve away. And for the briefest of moments, every last man at Shawshank felt free."[4]

Job must have experienced similar feelings of unspeakable joy and liberation as he finally soared free from the sickness, pain, depression, grief, and loneliness that had once imprisoned him. As his good health returned, his family grew, and his work prospered, he lived out his days as a fulfilled and blessed man.

After this, Job lived 140 years, and saw his sons and his grandsons, four generations. And Job died, an old man and full of days. (Job 42:16–17)

Most important, Job received God's stamp of approval: He passed the most extreme faith test with flying colors. He emerged blameless and victorious from the crucible of suffering.

What new discoveries about faith and trials have you made from your study of the book of Job?

NUGGETS OF WISDOM

Eugene Peterson writes about the mystery of God and the positive results that suffering brings into our lives:

> The mystery of God eclipses the darkness and the struggle. We realize that suffering calls *our* lives into question, not God's. The tables are turned: God-Alive is present to us. God is speaking to us. And so Job's experience is confirmed and repeated once again in our suffering and our vulnerable humanity.[5]

Losing possessions, financial resources, employees, children, and health all at once as Job did is certainly unusual. But losing one or more of these blessings over the course of a lifetime is not. In fact, we should expect that many aspects of our lives will change as we grow older, and that's scary at times.

Consider your possessions, your financial resources, your health, and the people you care about. Are any of these really secure? Just how vulnerable is your own humanity?

When (it is almost never a question of *if*, is it?) one or more of these are taken from your life, where will your security lie? Does your life have a foundation that will endure such a loss? If not, what can you do to prepare that foundation?

How have you already sensed God speaking to you through suffering in your life?

What's the most important lesson you've learned about suffering from the book of Job?

What's the most important lesson you've learned about yourself through this study? What have you learned about God and your faith in Him?

Saying good-bye to Job is like saying good-bye to an old friend. As we've studied his blameless character and his fire-refined life, we've grown to appreciate the legacy of faith that he has passed on to us. James wrote,

> Blessed is a man who perseveres under trial; for once he has been approved, he will receive the crown of life which the Lord has promised to those who love Him. (James 1:12)

As we have traced the steps of Job's journey, his remarkable story has become part of our lives. Taking the seeds of Job's experiences and planting them in our hearts equips us with biblical principles and vital faith lessons that will bring forth fruit when we endure similar trials. Now, press forward with renewed faith and confidence, keeping your eyes on that crown of life that God has promised you!

Endnotes

Chapter 1

Unless otherwise noted below, all material in this chapter is based on or quoted from Charles R. Swindoll, "Setting the Stage for Disaster," a sermon in Job, *March 3, 2002.*

1. Taken from *Disappointment with God*—Hardcover by Phillip D. Yancey. Copyright © 1988 by Phillip Yancey. Used by permission of Zondervan.

2. Elmer B. Smick, "Job," *Zondervan NIV Bible Commentary,* vol. 1, eds. Kenneth L. Barker and John R. Kohlenberger III (Grand Rapids, Mich.: Zondervan Publishing House, 1994), 746.

3. Geoffrey W. Bromiley, ed. *The International Standard Bible Encyclopedia,* vol. 4 (Grand Rapids, Mich.: William B. Eerdmans Publishing Company, 1988), 340, 342.

Chapter 2

Unless otherwise noted below, all material in this chapter is based on or quoted from Charles R. Swindoll, "Reeling and Recovering from Devastating News," a sermon in Job, *March 10, 2002.*

1. Yancey, *Disappointment with God,* 163–4.

2. Bromiley, *International Standard Bible Encyclopedia,* vol. 2, 80.

3. Adapted from Lisa Beamer, *Let's Roll* (Wheaton: Tyndale House Publishers, Inc., 2002), 211–14.

4. Henry Wadsworth Longfellow, "The Ladder of St. Augustine."

5. Barker and Kohlenberger, eds., *Zondervan NIV Bible Commentary,* 742.

6. Charles R. Swindoll, from the sermon entitled "Released in Order to Obey," as quoted in *Paul: A Man of Grace and Grit* (Nashville: W Publishing Group, 2002), 123.

7. Corrie ten Boom, as quoted by Charles R. Swindoll in *Living Above the Level of Mediocrity* (Waco, TX.: Word Books, 1987), 114.

Chapter 3

Unless otherwise noted below, all material in this chapter is based on or quoted from Charles R. Swindoll, "Satan vs. Job . . . Round Two," a sermon in Job, *March 24, 2002.*

1. *Merriam-Webster's Collegiate Dictionary,* 10th ed., s.v. "dualism."

2. Charles Dyer and Gene Merrill, *The Old Testament Explorer* (Nashville: Word Publishing, 2001), 378.

3. Merrill F. Unger, *The New Unger's Bible Dictionary* (Chicago: Moody Press, 1985), 1133. Used by permission.

4. John F. Walvoord and Roy B. Zuck, *The Bible Knowledge Commentary,* (Colorado Springs, Colo: Victor Books, 1985), 721.

5. Walvoord and Zuck, *Bible Knowledge Commentary,* 721.

6. Warren Wiersbe, *Be Patient: Waiting on God in Difficult Times* (Colorado Springs, Colo.: Chariot Victor Publishing, 1991), 19.

7. "Change My Heart, O God," Eddie Espinosa, © 1982 Mercy/Vineyard Publishing (ASCAP). All rights reserved. Used by permission.

8. Walvoord and Zuck, *Bible Knowledge Commentary,* 721.

Chapter 4

Unless otherwise noted below, all material in this chapter is based on or quoted from Charles R. Swindoll, "Job's Advice to Friends," a sermon in Job, April 7, 2002.

1. *Merriam-Webster's Collegiate Dictionary,* s.v. "crucible."
2. Walvoord and Zuck, *Bible Knowledge Commentary,* 722.
3. Walvoord and Zuck, *Bible Knowledge Commentary,* 722.
4. Eugene H. Peterson, "Introduction to Job," *The Message: The Bible in Contemporary Language* (Colorado Springs: NavPress, 2002), 840.
5. "Blessed Be Your Name," Matt Redman and Beth Redman, © 2002 Thank You Music, administered by EMI Christian Music Publishers. All rights reserved. Used by permission.
6. Les Parrott and Leslie Parrott, "Go Ahead, Get Closer . . .," *Marriage Partnership,* Fall 2003. Adapted from Les and Leslie Parrott, *The Love List* (Grand Rapids: Zondervan Publishing House, 2002).

Chapter 5

Unless otherwise noted below, all material in this chapter is based on or quoted from Charles R. Swindoll, "The Mournful Wail of a Miserable Man," a sermon in Job, April 14, 2002.

1. Reprinted by permission of Harvard Business School Press. From *The Art of Possibility: Transforming Professional and Personal Life* by Rosamund Stone Zander and Benjamin Zander. Boston, MA 2002, pp. 44–45. Copyright © 2002 by Rosamund Zander and Benjamin Zander. All rights reserved.
2. F. F. Bruce, ed., *The International Bible Commentary* (Grand Rapids: Zondervan Publishing House, 1986), 524.
3. Walvoord and Zuck, *Bible Knowledge Commentary,* 722–23.
4. Walvoord and Zuck, *Bible Knowledge Commentary,* 723.
5. Walvoord and Zuck, *Bible Knowledge Commentary,* 723.
6. Charles Haddon Spurgeon, "The Minister's Fainting Fits," *Lectures to My Students* (Grand Rapids: Zondervan Publishing House, 1970), 155–56.
7. Yancey, *Disappointment with God,* 172–73.

Chapter 6

Unless otherwise noted below, all material in this chapter is based on or quoted from Charles R. Swindoll, "Responding to Bad Counsel," a sermon in Job, April 21, 2002.

1. *Merriam-Webster's Collegiate Dictionary,* s. v. "syllogism."
2. Walvoord and Zuck, *Bible Knowledge Commentary,* 725.
3. Jeff VanVonderan, *Tired of Trying to Measure Up* (Minneapolis: Bethany House Publishers, 1989), 16.

Chapter 7

Unless otherwise noted below, all material in this chapter is based on or quoted from Charles R. Swindoll, "Continuing the Verbal Fistfight," a sermon in Job, April 28, 2002.

1. Reprinted by permission of Thomas Nelson, Inc., Nashville, TN, from the book entitled *The Sacred Romance,* copyright 1997 by Brent Curtis and John Eldredge. All rights reserved.
2. Curtis and Eldredge, *Sacred Romance,* 23.
3. Henry Louis Mencken, http:watchfuleye.com/mencken.html.

Endnotes

4. Elmer B. Smick, "Job," *The Expositor's Bible Commentary,* vol. 4 (Grand Rapids: Zondervan Publishing House, 1991), 905–06.

5. William Henry Green, *Conflict and Triumph: The Argument of the Book of Job Unfolded* (Carlisle, Penn.: The Banner of Truth Trust, 1999), 54–55. Used by permission.

6. Oliver Wendell Holmes, as quoted at http://home.att/net/~quotations/friendship.html.

7. Henry James, as quoted at http://quotes.prolix.nu/Humanity.

Chapter 8

Unless otherwise noted below, all material in this chapter is based on or quoted from Charles R. Swindoll, "When Rebuke and Resistance Collide," a sermon in Job, *May 2, 2002.*

1. Wiersbe, *Be Patient,* 46.
2. Wiersbe, *Be Patient,* 46.
3. Thomas à Kempis, as quoted in Wiersbe, *Be Patient,* 56.
4. Wiersbe, *Be Patient,* 47.
5. Reprinted from *The Pressure's Off.* Copyright © 2002 by Lawrence Crabb, Jr., Ph.D., P.C. Waterbrook Press, Colo. All rights reserved. Used by permission, 183.
6. Charles R. Swindoll, *Intimacy with the Almighty: Encountering Christ in the Secret Places of Your Life* (Nashville: J. Countryman, 1999), 15, 20. Used by permission of J. Countryman, a division of Thomas Nelson, Inc.
7. Unger, *The New Unger's Bible Dictionary,* 550–51.

Chapter 9

Unless otherwise noted below, all material in this chapter is based on or quoted from Charles R. Swindoll, "Graceless Words for a Grieving Man," a sermon in Job, *May 26, 2002.*

1. Wiersbe, *Be Patient,* 56.
2. Stephen R. Covey, *The Seven Habits of Highly Effective People* (New York: Simon and Schuster, 1989), 30–31.
3. C. Gene Wilkes, "Extreme Love # 6: Love Your Neighbor," http://www.lifeway.com.
4. Yancey, *Disappointment with God,* 203–4.

Chapter 10

Unless otherwise noted below, all material in this chapter is based on or quoted from Charles R. Swindoll, "Reassuring Hope for the Assaulted and Abused," a sermon in Job, *June 9, 2002.*

1. Motivational-Depot, quoted by Nancy McFadden, http://www.mcfaddenseminars.com/friendship-quotes.htm.
2. Mother Teresa, as quoted at Graham's Homepage, http://www.weeks-g.dircon.co.uk/quotes_k.htm.
3. Wiersbe, *Be Patient,* 74.
4. George Frederic Handel, *Messiah,* Libretto, Part III, http://www.messiah.com/Information/about_The_Messiah/Libretto/libretto.html.
5. Wiersbe, *Be Patient,* 75.

ENDNOTES

Chapter 11

All material in this chapter is based on or quoted from Charles R. Swindoll "Responding Wisely When Falsely Accused," a sermon in Job, *June 23, 2002.*

Chapter 12

Unless otherwise noted below, all material in this chapter is based on or quoted from Charles R. Swindoll "How to Handle Criticism with Class," a sermon in Job, *July 14, 2002.*

1. Ernest Hemingway, quoted at www.great-quotes.com (accessed June 5, 2003).
2. From *Churchill on Leadership* by Steven F. Hayward, copyright © 1997 by Steven F. Hayward. Used by permission of Prima Publishing, a division of Random House, Inc., 121–22.
3. *Merriam-Webster's Collegiate Dictionary,* s. v. "Hypocrite."
4. Wiersbe, *Be Patient,* 91.
5. Taken from *Elijah: A Man Like Us,* © 1998 by David Roper. Used by permission of Discovery House Publishers, Box 3566, Grand Rapids, MI 49501. All rights reserved.

Chapter 13

Unless otherwise noted below, all material in this chapter is based on or quoted from Charles R. Swindoll "The Futility of Unscrewing the Inscrutable," sermon in Job, *July 21, 2002.*

1. *Merriam-Webster's Collegiate Dictionary,* s. v. "inscrutable."
2. Wiersbe, *Be Patient,* 100.
3. Wiersbe, *Be Patient,* 102.
4. Wiersbe, *Be Patient,* 103.
5. Smick, "Job," *Zondervan NIV Bible Commentary,* vol. 1, 744–45.
6. Charles R. Swindoll, *Come Before Winter . . . And Share My Hope* (Wheaton, Ill.: Living Books, Tyndale House Publishers, Inc., 1985) 462–63.
7. Excerpts of 184 words from pp. 1, 8 from *The Knowledge of the Holy; The Attributes of God: Their Meaning in the Christian Life* by A. W. Tozer. Copyright © 1961 by Aiden Wilson Tozer. Reprinted by permission of HarperCollins Publishers, Inc.

Chapter 14

Unless otherwise noted below, all material in this chapter is based on or quoted from Charles R. Swindoll, "A Recommitment to Things That Matter," a sermon in Job, *September 15, 2002.*

1. John Piper, *Brothers, We Are Not Professionals: A Plea to Pastors for Radical Ministry* (Nashville: Broadman & Holman Publishers, 2002), ix. Used by permission.
2. Wiersbe, *Be Patient,* 102–3.
3. *Merriam-Webster's Collegiate Dictionary,* s. v. "imprecate."
4. Wiersbe, *Be Patient,* 105.
5. Tozer, *Knowledge of the Holy,* 1.

Endnotes

Chapter 15

Unless otherwise noted below, all material in this chapter is based on or quoted from Charles R. Swindoll, "The Passionate Testimony of an Innocent Man," a sermon in Job, *September 22, 2002.*

1. Alan Simpson, as quoted in Robert J. Lloyd, "Minute Meditations: Integrity" for June 2001, (http://www.tidings.org/minutes/minute200106.htm, accessed November 20, 2003).

2. Wiersbe, *Be Patient,* 110–11.

3. From *The Gospel According to Job* by Mike Mason. Copyright © 1994, p. 315. Used by permission of Crossway Books, a division of Good News Publishers, Wheaton, Ill. 60817.

4. Bromiley, *International Standard Bible Encyclopedia,* vol. 1, 614.

Chapter 16

Unless otherwise noted below, all material in this chapter is based on or quoted from Charles R. Swindoll, "Another Long-Winded Monologue," a sermon in Job, *September 29, 2002.*

1. David Atkinson, *The Message of Job: Suffering and Grace* (Downers Grove, Ill.: InterVarsity Press, 1991), 122.

2. Atkinson, *The Message of Job,* 122.

3. C. S. Lewis, as quoted by Warren Wiersbe in *Be Patient: Waiting on God in Difficult Times* (Colorado Springs, Colo.: Chariot Victor Publishing, 1991), p. 127.

4. Wiersbe, *Be Patient,* 129 (my italics).

Chapter 17

Unless otherwise noted below, all material in this chapter is based on or quoted from Charles R. Swindoll, "A Penetrating Reproof from the Almighty," a sermon in Job, *October 6, 2002.*

1. Martin Luther, as quoted by Philip Schaff in *History of the Christian Church,* vol. 7, *Modern Christianity: The German Reformation,* 2d ed., rev. (Grand Rapids, Mich.: William B. Eerdmans Publishing Co., 1910), 112. Used by permission.

2. Martin Luther, quoted in Schaff, *History of the Christian Church,* 116.

3. Wiersbe, *Be Patient,* 144.

4. Tom Anderson, quoted in Gary Inrig, *True North* (Grand Rapids, Mich.: Discovery House Publishers, 2002), 142–43.

Chapter 18

Unless otherwise noted below, all material in this chapter is based on or quoted from Charles R. Swindoll, "Full Repentance for All the Right Reasons" a sermon in Job, *October 20, 2002.*

1. Mason, *The Gospel According to Job,* 413.

2. Mason, *The Gospel According to Job,* 416.

3. Smick, "Job," *Zondervan Bible Commentary,* vol. 1, 787–88.

4. John E. Hartley, *The Book of Job* (Grand Rapids, Mich.: William B. Eerdmans Publishing Company, 1988), 537. Used by permission.

5. Charles Spurgeon, as quoted by Warren Wiersbe in *Be Patient: Waiting on God in Difficult Times* (Colorado Springs, Colo.: Chariot Victor Publishing, 1991), p. 153.

ENDNOTES

Chapter 19

Unless otherwise noted below, all material in this chapter is based on or quoted from Charles R. Swindoll, "Finally, God's Justice Rolls Down," a sermon in Job, *October 27, 2002.*

1. Charles A. Beard, as quoted at http://www.wisdomquotes.com/001835.html.

Chapter 20

Unless otherwise noted below, all material in this chapter is based on or quoted from Charles R. Swindoll, "And Job Lived Happily Ever After . . . Or Did He?" a sermon in Job, *November 3, 2002.*

1. Mason, *The Gospel According to Job,* 441.
2. Hartley, *The Book of Job,* 543.
3. Mason, *The Gospel According to Job,* 443.
4. Wiersbe, *Be Patient,* 154.
5. Mason, *The Gospel According to Job,* 445.
6. Source unknown, "A 17th Century Nun's Prayer" as quoted by Dale Evans Rogers in *Time Out, Ladies,* Fleming H. Revell Company, 1966.

Chapter 21

Unless otherwise noted below, all material in this chapter is based on or quoted from Charles R. Swindoll, "What Job Teaches Us about Ourselves," a sermon in Job, *November 10, 2002.*

1. Atkinson, *The Message of Job,* 13.
2. Charles Schultz, *Peanuts,* quoted at http://www.dashhouse.com/sermons/1997/AM/970303.htm (accessed June 30, 2003).
3. Eugene Peterson, "Introduction to Job," *The Message,* 841–42.
4. Reprinted by Permission of Thomas Nelson, Inc., Nashville, TN, from the book entitled *Created to Be God's Friend,* copyright © 1999 by Henry T. Blackaby. All rights reserved.
5. Benjamin Zander and Rosamund Stone Zander, *The Art of Possibility* (Boston: Harvard Business School Press, 2000), 118–19.
6. Friedrich Nietzsche, quoted in Eugene H. Peterson, *A Long Obedience in the Same Direction: Discipleship in an Instant Society* (Downers Grove, Ill.: InterVarsity Press, 2000).

Chapter 22

Unless otherwise noted below, all material in this chapter is based on or quoted from Charles R. Swindoll, "What Job Teaches Us about Our God," a sermon in Job, *November 17, 2002.*

1. Quotations Network, http://www.quotesandjokes.com/jokes/computerjokes.html (accessed on November 24, 2003).
2. Hartley, *The Book of Job,* 535–36.
3. Yancey, *Disappointment with God,* 189–91.
4. Ken Gire, *The Reflective Life: Becoming More Spiritually Sensitive to the Everyday Moments of Life* (Colorado Springs, Colo.: Chariot Victor Publishing, 1998), 171. Used by permission.
5. Peterson, "Introduction to Job," *The Message,* 842.

Books for Probing Further

WE HOPE YOU'VE ENJOYED DIGGING MORE DEEPLY into the mysteries of God as you've walked alongside Job on his spiritual journey. Job suffered tremendously, yet he remained faithful. As a result, God poured out a wealth of blessings on him that he never could have anticipated.

We pray that you will emerge from your past, present, and future trials as a stronger, more faithful, spiritually blessed individual. The following books will encourage you to keep pressing on despite the painful obstacles you encounter. Select a few resources from the list and enjoy them. The truths they contain will help you to keep your spiritual priorities straight and remain steadfast in Christ, the author and perfecter of our faith (Heb. 12:2).

Atkinson, David. *The Message of Job: Suffering and Grace.* Downers Grove, Ill.: InterVarsity Press, 1991.

Barker, Kenneth L. and John R. Kohlenberger III, eds. *The Zondervan NIV Bible Commentary.* Volume 1: Old Testament. Grand Rapids, Mich.: Zondervan Publishing House, 1994.

Chambers, Oswald. *Baffled to Fight Better: Job and the Problem of Suffering.* Grand Rapids, Mich.: Discovery House Publishers, 1990.

Dell, Katharine. *Shaking a Fist at God: Struggling with the Mystery of Undeserved Suffering.* Chicago: Triumph Books, 1997.

Gire, Ken. *The Weathering Grace of God: The Beauty God Brings from Life's Upheavals.* Ann Arbor, Mich.: Vine Books, 2001.

Hartley, John E. *The Book of Job.* Grand Rapids, Mich.: William B. Eerdmans Publishing Company, 1988.

Komp, Diane M., M.D. *Why Me? A Doctor Looks at the Book of Job.* Downers Grove, Ill.: InterVarsity Press, 2001.

Lewis, C. S. *The Problem of Pain.* San Francisco: Harper SanFrancisco, 2001.

Mason, Mike. *The Gospel According to Job.* Wheaton, Ill.: Crossway Books, 1994.

Peterson, Eugene. *The Message: The Bible in Contemporary Language,* Colorado Springs: NavPress, 2002.

Rader, Dick and Sue. *A Road Beyond the Suffering: An Experiential Journey Through the Book of Job.* Franklin, Tenn.: Providence House Publishers, 1997.

Vanauken, Sheldon. *A Severe Mercy.* San Francisco: Harper SanFrancisco, 1992.

Wiersbe, Warren. *Be Patient: Waiting on God in Difficult Times.* Colorado Springs: Chariot Victor Publishing, 1993.

Yancey, Phillip. *Disappointment with God.* Grand Rapids, Mich.: Zondervan Publishing House, 1988.

Zuck, Roy B., ed. *Sitting with Job: Selected Studies on the Book of Job.* Grand Rapids, Mich.: Baker Book House, 1992.